MW01132875

The Eastern Shore Baseball League

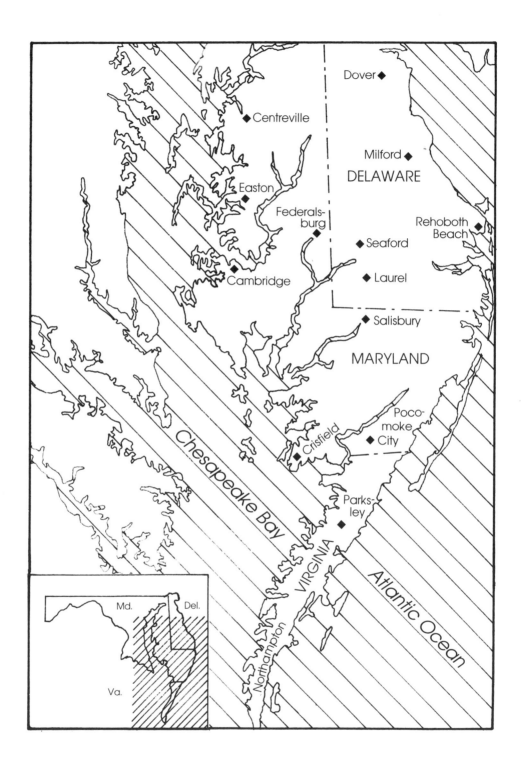

Dover ◆

Centreville ◆

Milford ◆

DELAWARE

Easton ◆

Federals-
burg ◆

Rehoboth
Beach ◆

◆ Seaford

Cambridge ◆

◆ Laurel

◆ Salisbury

MARYLAND

Poco-
moke
◆ City

Crisfield ◆

Chesapeake Bay

Parks-
ley ◆

VIRGINIA

Atlantic Ocean

Northampton

Md.   Del.

Va.

THE
EASTERN
SHORE
BASEBALL
LEAGUE

by

William W. Mowbray

TIDEWATER PUBLISHERS

CENTREVILLE MARYLAND

Library of Congress Cataloging-in-Publication Data

Mowbray, William W.
    The Eastern Shore Baseball League / by William W. Mowbray.—1st ed.
      p. cm.
    Includes index.
    ISBN 0-87033-394-1
    1. Eastern Shore Baseball League—History. 2. Baseball players—United States—Biography. 3. Baseball—Eastern Shore (Md. and Va.)—Records. I. Title.
GV875.E27M69 1989
796.357′060752′1—dc19
                                        88-32224
                                            CIP

Manufactured in the United States of America
First edition

To Calvin W. Mowbray, Sr.
March 6, 1914 – July 5, 1988

Contents

Preface

I REMEMBER the first time my father took me outside to "have a catch." The very first ball he tossed struck me in the forehead and I've been in love with the game of baseball ever since.

I grew up on the Eastern Shore of Maryland when baseball was still a game for kids. It was fun. We didn't need uniforms, fancy equipment, parks, or the Supreme Court to tell us how to play the game. We didn't need parents, coaches, managers, or money. We didn't need statistics, sponsors, queens, parades, and all-star teams to play baseball—and have a great time doing it. In my opinion, organized youth sports of today tend to parallel unions and bureaucracies in that their good intentions are admirable, but the end results debatable.

In 1946 baseball ranked just ahead of Abbott and Costello, Roy Rogers and Gene Autry, the Rocketman serial, marbles, scooters, Charlie Chan, the Bowery Boys, Captain Midnight, Gangbusters, climbing trees, and fishing, and was way ahead of girls.

I was born, raised, and still live on the Delmarva Peninsula—right next to the Chesapeake Bay, one of the largest estuaries in the world. Most persons not born and raised in this area are led to believe that Ocean City, crabs, waterfowl, and marsh are all that exist in this magnificent region. There are, however, many additional aspects of living in this noble land,

and one of these was the Eastern Shore Baseball League—a Class D professional league that operated for 15 years with a working agreement with major league baseball.

I'm sure there must have been some social dilemmas of significance during the postwar year of 1946, but I was not aware of any. What *did* come to our town of Cambridge in 1946 was baseball, and in a way I had never seen. Swimming in the Choptank River and sandlot baseball games were near the top of my list of priorities; but now Carlton Benny, baseball's greatest (but least-remembered) promoter, was driving up and down every street in Cambridge announcing by means of two loud-speakers temporarily attached to the roof of his car, "Baseball, baseball tonight!" And I realized that Cambridge's Dodger Park was the place to be in the cool summer evenings when our own personal connection with *the* Brooklyn Dodgers was playing at home—a real live professional baseball team right here in Cambridge, *our* team!

It never occurred to me that professional baseball in the form of the Eastern Shore League had been here on two previous occasions. And it really didn't matter, because the Cambridge Canners and the Cambridge Cardinals had gone out of existence before I was born. But the Dodgers—I couldn't wait to get to the park and see my heroes: Chris Van Cuyk, Stew Hofferth, Bob Stramm, Mike Quill, Gene Kern, Charley Tim Thompson, Goldy Tyler, Phil Lewandowski, Don Zimmer, Gale Wade, Carroll Beringer, Bert Hamric, Don Nicholas, Joe Pignatano, and my favorite, Zeke Zeisz. (There was just something about that name—Zeke Zeisz. Never could figure out why he didn't make it to the Hall of Fame—or the major leagues, for that matter.)

From 1946 to 1949 it was me and the Dodgers. Some sportswriters had the gall to call our team the "Little Dodgers." There was nothing little to me about the Cambridge Dodgers except Don Nicholas. So what if they finished dead last in '46? The fact remains that a love affair developed during that summer of 1946. The Choptank River, sandlot baseball, and the Dodgers—what else could a six-year-old ask for?

(I don't bleed Dodger blue anymore. The move to L.A. was too much for this Dodgers fan.)

When the ESL folded for the final time in 1949, for some reason (probably the logo) I became a Cleveland Indians fan and idolized Al Rosen. I also rooted for the Washington Senators (when they were not playing the Indians) because whenever my mother wrote for tickets up at Griffith Stadium we always got the seats we asked for—box seats, front

Name	Position	Bats	Throws
Feinberg, Edward	2B	Both	R
Born-Place	Date		Married
Philadelphia,Pa.	9-20-18	Height	Weight
Address		6'	190
Philadelp ia,Pa.			

Teams Played With

Centreville 6/37-38-rel.to Phila.NL 3/38-rel.to
Montgomery 3/38-rec.by Phila.NL 8/38-39-opt.to
Pensacola 4/39-ret.to Phila.NL 5/39-opt.to Scranton 5/39-ret.to Phila.NL 7/39-opt.to Rocky Mount
7/39- opt.to St.Paul 7/39- ret.to Phila. NL 8/39-
rel.8/39-Springfield,Mass.10/39-Greenville,S.C.
4/40- Vol.ret.1940-41-42-43-rein.5/43-Free agent
5/43-

Documentation of a player's movement in professional baseball was gathered by use of index data cards for research purposes by the author. Sample card shown is of Ed Feinberg.

row, next to the visitors' dugout. At one time I had three autograph books complete with every Cleveland Indian signature from 1952 through 1954.

My Uncle Roy took me to see a couple of International League games in Baltimore and, of course, when the St. Louis Browns franchise moved east in 1954, I adopted the Baltimore Orioles as my favorite team out of state loyalty. But it wasn't until Rosen retired that I totally gave up on the Indians.

Although I doubt it will have much influence on the future of Delmarva, perhaps I can at least contribute a footnote on a neglected aspect of our history. One of the purposes of this book is to provide a historical account of the Eastern Shore League. It is primarily concerned with those persons associated with the ESL who made it to the major leagues. I've also included those Delmarva natives who made it to the big leagues although they did not play in the ESL.

Actually this work was not my original intention, but the result of a series of events spanning 20 years. After graduating from Florida Southern College in 1966 I became sports editor of the Cambridge *Daily Banner*. One of the first stories I wrote was about a friend of mine named Crawford Foxwell. "Crab" has been a sports memorabilia collector for many years and he rekindled my interest in the ESL. A few years later I hired a young fellow named Barry Sparks and had him do a weekly column with emphasis on local sports history. He did a wonderful four-part series on the Eastern Shore League and, with his permission, I have used some of his research in preparing this book.

But it was on a flight with the Baltimore Colts in the late sixties that John Steadman suggested I gather all my research on the ESL and put it together for a book. And so here we are. I hope it is as much fun to read as it was to gather the information and that it jogs the memory for you as it does for me of a time when baseball was just plain fun.

Special thanks go to my family, especially Belle Wilkinson Mowbray, who escorted me to my first professional baseball game in 1946 to see the Class D Cambridge Dodgers (thus addicting me for life to the great game of baseball), and to Crawford Foxwell, Russ Frazier, Claude Gootee, Jeff Kernan, Bob Layton, Ernie Leap, Paul MacFarlane, the late Ed Nichols, John F. Pardon, Hal Smeltzly, Barry Sparks, John Steadman, and to all former Eastern Shore Leaguers, wherever they may be. Zeke Zeisz, where are you?

Part I

History

Homer Smoot

CHAPTER 1

Introduction

MOST EXPERTS agree baseball was introduced in the United States in about 1846, and professional baseball players began to be paid in 1869 with the formation of the Cincinnati Red Stockings. Cincinnati decided to pay its players for one reason: to be able to field the best team and hopefully win the most games. The early economic aspect has not changed.

But baseball, like the ESL, struggled in the early years. Several leagues formed and disbanded, a number of organizations became involved and then disappeared and some scandals were associated with the sport.

The American League started out in 1894 as the Western Association and was regarded as a minor league, but by 1903 there were two major leagues, American and National, and the first World Series was held.

As the game of baseball progressed, the major league teams started forming "working agreements" with the minor leagues for the purpose of developing future major league ballplayers. Today, almost all minor league teams are dependent on the financial backing of a major league club.

Some of the earlier minor leagues were the California League, South Atlantic League, Cotton State League, Tri-State League, South West

Texas League, Pacific Coast League, Southern League, and Ohio State League. The International League of today (a AAA league) began in 1884 when it was known as the Eastern League. The American Association and the Texas Leagues began in 1902.

Records of the old minor leagues are difficult to come by. They were not included in the major league baseball "guides" of the day and often results were not included in newspaper accounts.

Perhaps the most obvious difference between the minors of yesteryear and today is that many early minor league players had no desire to become major league players, an attitude unheard-of today. The reason was usually of a geographic nature. A ballplayer was quite content to play in a minor league located near his home or in the pleasant warmth of the West Coast or the South.

Professional baseball players have not always enjoyed the adulation and hero worship modern ballplayers receive today. The fact is that in the early 1900s playing baseball for a living was not a very respectable occupation. The average working person considered baseball players bums, too lazy to work for a living. Playing a game was simply not acceptable as a definition of an honest day's work. The million-dollar-a-year baseball players of today, believe it or not, in the early days were referred to as rascals and scalawags.

Eventually the minor leagues became stepping-stones to the majors. They were labeled Classes D, C, B, and A. Today they have evolved into the rookie leagues, Classes A, AA, and AAA.

Tracing the introduction of organized, professional baseball on the Eastern Shores of Maryland and Virginia is an almost impossible assignment, but there is sufficient documentation of semiprofessional teams operating in some semblance of a genuine league dating back to at least the earliest 1900s.

And we have found evidence of at least one attempt of Shore persons to form an official league in that era. A letter dated June 6, 1911, from A. B. Burris, Ray Truitt, and R. V. Rich of Salisbury to Capt. James B. Harris of Cambridge read:

> We are writing to get your ideas as to the formation of a baseball league composed of the towns on the Eastern Shore of Maryland and lower Delaware. Our idea is to give the teams the privilege of hiring not more than three or four men, the balance of the team to be composed of residents of the county in which the town is situated.

4

If you would care to form a league under such conditions, or if you have any suggestions to make, we would be glad to hear from you.

Would it be convenient for you to send a representative to confer with those of other clubs at some point that would be most convenient to all concerned?

Your prompt reply will be greatly appreciated.

It is interesting to note that in this letter the "hiring" of players is undisguised, thus theoretically eliminating future accusations of previous teams' utilizing "ringers" for important games, and also suggesting a "professional" league.

Immediately upon receipt of the letter, Capt. Harris, president of the Cambridge Baseball Club, scheduled a public meeting for June 11 at the Masonic Temple in Cambridge for all interested parties to discuss the proposal. Also in attendance at the meeting were Vernon S. Bradley, secretary, and Charles Mace, treasurer, of the Cambridge club.

No official minor league came to be as a result of this early attempt.

The basic framework of the old minor leagues and those of today revolves primarily around the International League, the American Association, the Southern Association, the Texas League, and the Pacific Coast League. All these leagues are still active today after having started in the early 1900s.

The Eastern Shore League was finally born in 1922 and until its final year of 1949 it operated as a Class D league.

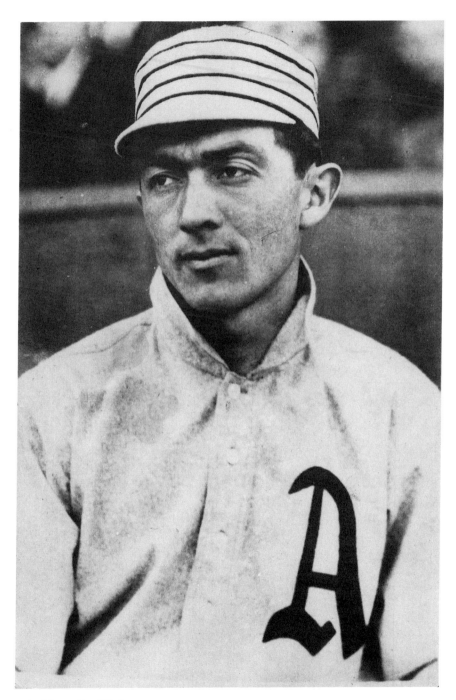

Frank "Home Run" Baker

CHAPTER 2

Pre-League Activity

S INCE THEY ARE recognized as the origin of the professional Eastern Shore League we will first briefly consider the semipro town teams that flourished on Delmarva, one of which was the Cambridge Baseball Club, established in 1905.

In addition to competing against numerous other town teams on the Shore the Cambridge Club exhibited a semblance of authenticity by scheduling exhibition games with outside opponents such as Towson (Baltimore Suburban League), Mt. Washington Baseball Club, and even a barnstorming squad named the Nebraska Indians, which was composed of a group of native American Indians.

Town teams had existed in varying forms even prior to 1905, and the Eastern Shore's first contribution to the major leagues was Homer Smoot of Galestown, Md. There has been no record found of Homer's participation with a town team, but we know he spent five years in the major leagues with the Cardinals and Reds from 1902 to 1906.

These makeshift town baseball teams on the Eastern Shore brought into being many heated rivalries, which have to varying degrees carried over to this day both in and out of the sports arenas, particularly among the "big cities" of Cambridge, Easton, and Salisbury. Attendance at these

Jimmie Foxx

amateur or semipro games on occasion exceeded the total population of the towns they were being played in.

Perhaps the reason for this phenomenon was the fact that another homegrown product, Frank "Home Run" Baker of Trappe, Md., was making his major league debut in 1908. But a more likely explanation is that baseball was probably the best available form of entertainment for Delmarva citizens after a hard day in the field or on the water.

All sorts of quasi-Eastern Shore Leagues operated for the next 10 years or so and still another pair of local products ascended to the major leagues. Vic Keen of Snow Hill, Md., debuted with the Athletics in 1918 and Huck Betts of Millsboro, Del., commenced his rookie season with the Phillies in 1920.

Concurrently, it was during the Golden Age of Sports, the fabulous Roaring Twenties, that bona fide official endorsement of that tenacious dream of Shore baseball fans—an authentic professional baseball league recognized by major league baseball—finally came to be.

The United States bought the Virgin Islands in 1916, the joint Congressional resolution declaring peace with Germany, Austria, and Hungary was signed by President Harding in 1921, and *Reader's Digest* was founded in 1922. On June 12, 1922, the official opening game of the professional Eastern Shore League began play.

CHAPTER 3

The First Class D Professional Eastern Shore League

(1922 ♦ 1927)

*I*N MAY 1921 the Salisbury Chamber of Commerce favored the formation of a six-team professional baseball league on the Eastern Shore (more accurately, on Delmarva, since Seaford and Dover, Del., were initially included as two of the target cities).

Unlike the 1911 proposal, a recommendation was made that each town post a $1,000 forfeit fee as its guarantee to host a minor league club. The proposed original six cities were: Cambridge, Centreville, Chestertown, Crisfield, and Salisbury of Maryland; and Dover and/or Seaford of Delaware. J. Vincent Jamison, president of the Blue Ridge League, was engaged to meet with local representatives to explain the working details of organized professional baseball and the particulars of operating a Class D League.

It was announced October 13, 1921, that the newly formed Eastern Shore League would begin official operation as a Class D professional minor league for the 1922 season. The original teams in the neophyte league were admitted based on a geographical concept utilizing Salisbury (the largest city on the Eastern Shore) as the hub of a wheel, anticipating travel efficiency and a continuation of natural rivalries of the previous amateur town teams. As a result of this configuration four (Centreville,

Chestertown, Seaford, and Dover) of the original recommended six cities were deleted from the new league. Easton also applied for admission to the league in 1922, but the request was denied because league officials felt the city was located too far north of the central city of Salisbury.

Members of the original Eastern Shore League of 1922 were Cambridge, Crisfield, Pocomoke City, and Salisbury, Md.; Laurel, Del.; and Parksley, Va.

Laurel, Parksley, and Pocomoke City were contacted by league officials and asked to join the league since they had existing parks; the three towns wasted little time paying the required entrance fee to complete the first professional baseball league on Delmarva.

It is intriguing to note that the original league member cities did not adopt their parent major league affiliates' nicknames, but instead utilized appellations which directly paralleled each city's own unique geographical and cultural heritage, for instance, the Cambridge Canners, the Parksley Spuds, and the Laurel Blue Hens.

Salisbury and Cambridge would ultimately be the only two original cities to conclusively survive the three distinct phases of the ESL that totalled 15 years of operation over a span of 28 years under the auspices of major league baseball.

The first six participating cities posted $875 each and were instructed by major league baseball to build new ballparks or renovate existing parks to meet professional standards.

President-elect Walter B. Miller of Salisbury officially opened Eastern Shore League play June 12, 1922, with a total of over 6,000 fans attending the three opening games. An ill omen unfortunately occurred during the opening game held in Parksley, Va., as an irate fan leaped from the grandstand during the game with Crisfield, voiced his personal opinion of a disputed call, and physically attacked the umpire, who had to be hospitalized. (Rowdiness of Eastern Shore fans is noted elsewhere in this history, particularly during the 1937–41 period.)

Still, the initial season was an effective one for the newborn league. A future major leaguer and hometown product of Cambridge, Jake Flowers hit a solid .312 with 14 home runs for the Canners, who were managed by Herb Armstrong. Armstrong was player/manager (a frequent arrangement throughout ESL history) for the Canners, appearing in 67 games and hitting .249 in the initial season.

Manager Armstrong's Canners finished second in the 1922 season behind the champion Parksley Spuds. The following account of the first

Cambridge Ball Park, *circa* 1922. Prominent area men entertain base-ball notables. *Standing (l. to r.):* W. Carl Bradley; Robert H. Matthews, Sr.; Calvin Harrington, Sr.; Ban Johnson, Pres., American Baseball League; Samuel W. Lithicum; Ex-Gov. Emerson C. Harrington; Judge Josiah Bayley, of Salisbury; P. Watson Webb; (unidentified lad); Harry Rue, of Parksley, Va.; Dr. Brice W. Goldsborough; J. Vincent Jamison, Pres., Blue Ridge League. *Kneeling (l. to r.):* John Noble ———; L. D. T. Noble; Emmett Ewell; Frederick Stevens; Sidney H. Henry; ———; Daniel Wright; Frank Robbins. In the grandstand may be seen Messrs. Charles and Carroll Dill and Mr. and Mrs. Duncan Noble and young daughter, Jean (Mrs. William P. Chaffinch). Photograph loaned by Robert H. Matthews, Sr.

Cambridge Ball Park, circa 1922.

Eastern Shore League year was printed in *The Reach Official American League Guide*:

> Among the newcomers in the baseball field in 1922 was the Eastern Shore League. This was a fine six-club organization of clubs located in Laurel, De. and Parksley, Cambridge, Crisfield, Pocomoke and Salisbury, Md. The organizer was Mr. W.B. Miller of Salisbury, who also steered the organization through its initial season quite successfully. The season was comparatively short, running from June 12 to September 4. The race, though was spirited and exciting. Parksley winning out after a hard battle with Cambridge and Crisfield all the way.

There were three errors in that quote: First, Parksley is located in the state of Virginia; second, Pocomoke is correctly Pocomoke City; and third, Cambridge was hardly in the pennant chase, about which, more later.

Parksley boasted both the league batting and pitching champions that year with Fisher hitting .324 to top the league and Klingehoffer posting a 15–5 won-lost mound record.

Other notables of the independent shore leagues of the twenties, later to be involved with the official professional ESL, but absent from national media exposure, included Dallas Culver of Seaford, Del., (president of the ESL in 1948) who was a left-handed pitcher in the early twenties for the Laurel Blue Hens managed by Sam Frock. The most memorable day of his amateur career was in a game between Seaford and Federalsburg with one Frank Baker on the Federalsburg squad.

Culver retired the former four-time American League home run champion the first three times he faced him. But the fourth time, "Frank hit my best Sunday pitch out of the lot. I'll never forget it," said Culver.

Dr. Walter L. Grier of Milford, Del., (vice-president of the ESL in 1947) is credited by some with helping Jake Flowers and American League umpire Bill McGowan get their careers on the road.

"I paid Jake Flowers and Bill McGowan their first money ever earned on the ballfield," claimed Grier.

> It happened somewhere in the early twenties. Facing a tough game with the Dover club one Sunday, I called on my friend Coach Tom Kibler for some infield help.
> Milford had a great keystone combination that day. Jake Flowers at shortstop and Tom Kibler at second base. I knew Jake was ticketed for faster company the moment he fielded the first ground ball.

The story of McGowan dates back to 1914. McGowan wrote Dr. Grier and asked for a job umpiring. The letter was answered immediately: "I don't know anything about you, but will give you $5 to work a Dover-Milford game this weekend." And that was the start of McGowan's umpiring career, which in the course of time led to the major leagues.

Kibler, of course, would later lead the way in reorganizing the ESL in 1937, after it had folded in 1927, and in addition would serve as president of the league that year and be reelected president of the league for the 1946 and 1947 seasons. Known by his many friends and former players as both "The Colonel" and "Coach," he was a member of the independent shore league in 1908, playing for Cambridge.

And Hanson Horsey, who would later be umpire-in-chief of the ESL, pitched for the Seaford club in 1908.

John "Dutch" Brennan, superscout for the Philadelphia Athletics in 1947, following a scouting stint with the Brooklyn Dodgers in 1945 and 1946, had a brief fling with the 1922 Cambridge Canners and the following year started an umpiring career in the ESL. His baseball beginnings on the Eastern Shore were as a player in the independent league with the Queenstown club and also with Centreville and Salisbury from 1919 to 1921. Although he was a lifelong resident of Baltimore, he always referred to the Eastern Shore as his second home.

Oftentimes referred to as the archbishop of baseball scouts was one Charles "Pop" Kelchner. Pop scouted for the St. Louis Browns from 1912 to 1918 and then switched to the Cardinals. Two of his many discoveries were Eastern Shore Leaguers Danny Murtaugh and Jake Flowers as well as Cambridge-born Warren "Sheriff" Robinson who spent many years managing in the minor leagues before being promoted to a coaching position with the New York Mets.

A player who, without the shadow of a doubt, was one of the finest third basemen in the history of the game unfortunately performed "when only the ball was white" (a phrase used to describe the all-black leagues in the early days of baseball). William "Judy" Johnson triumphantly handled the hot corner for the Hilldale club out of Philadelphia from 1922 to 1929 and later was player/manager for the Homestead Greys and Pittsburgh Crawfords. Judy was no stranger to the ESL as a scout for the Philadelphia Phillies and finally was awarded his just tribute in 1975 when he was elected to the Baseball Hall of Fame. We Shore folks are also justly proud to claim Judy Johnson as one of our own as he was born in Snow Hill, Md.

Now back to that 1922 season and the ESL champion Parksley Spuds who, following their pennant title, were invited to participate in the first Five State Championship Series against the Blue Ridge League champion Martinsburg squad. Although the rookie Parksley team lost the series, the venture was considered a success since it generated much interest among the fans and turned out to be a major source of revenue for both leagues. Still, when the 1922 ESL balance sheet was completed it revealed a $3,500 deficit, excluding ground rents.

There were a number of explanations for the 1922 deficit, not the least of which was the practice of "cramming" a team in order to win a pennant near the end of the season—which brings us back to the third correction to *The Reach Guide*'s account of Parksley having a hard battle all of the way with Cambridge. The practice of "cramming" involved a team making a wholesale exchange of players in the last few weeks of the season to strengthen their stretch drive. During that 1922 season Cambridge utilized this practice and almost captured the pennant as they went from last place to second place in the final two weeks of the season. As a result the league passed the "August 1" rule at the conclusion of the season which prohibited trading of players after that date. Cambridge was hardly in the pennant chase at any other point in the season.

There was also the violation of the true basis of a Class D league concept—that of strict adherence to the salary limit, which at the time was $1,750 per month for a team. At least two teams in the 1922 league signed more than 50 candidates each during the season. The expense of one-way transportation for the surplus personnel, as well as their training costs, was borne by the management. This practice was slated to be eliminated in the 1923 season.

That first season also proved deficient with regard to yet another purpose of a Class D league—the development of young players to become major league material. Jake Flowers of Cambridge was the only 1922 ESLer to graduate to the major leagues.

Still, all considered, attendance throughout the league was surprisingly high, when taking into account the undersized population of the represented towns (the major characteristic of a Class D organization was that its cities represented an aggregate population of under 150,000), and the initial season proved to be an excellent forecast for future years.

Accordingly the overall feeling among officials, fans, and players toward the upcoming 1923 season was almost optimistic despite the financial situation being in the red from a year ago. For after all, 1922 had been the league's first attempt at organized professional baseball. A reporter probably summed up the optimism for the 1923 season best when he wrote,

> The enthusiasm for the national pastime has increased on the peninsula and it is now believed that the Eastern Shore League will remain active for many years. At least a majority of fans do not want to exchange organized baseball for the independent organizations supported by various towns prior to 1922.

During the winter of 1922 and the spring of 1923 Eastern Shore League club officials from each franchise were actively involved in cover-

These World-Famous Baseball Stars In Phillips Delicious Line-Up

The 1936 Cambridge city championship turned into a war between Coca-Cola and Phillips Delicious. By the final game of the series the Phillips Delicious team included these professional stars: back row (left to right), Frankie Hayes (Athletics), Dick Porter (Newark), Colonel Albanus Phillips, Jimmie Foxx (Boston Red Sox), W. Grason Winterbottom, Jimmie Deshong (Senators); front row, Oscar Roettger (Orioles), Henry Oana (Orioles), Billy Werber (Red Sox), Max Bishop (Athletics), and Roger Cramer (Red Sox).

ing the first year's deficit by selling additional stock to citizens. This was a common method of raising money under the working agreement that most clubs had with major league baseball. Under this working agreement the town baseball association was responsible for paying the salaries of the players, ranging from a limit of $1,750 per team per month in 1922 to $2,250 per team per month in 1947. The major league clubs would then pay approximately $2,000 for the exclusive rights to draft players from the Class D organization. Also on a working agreement basis the major league clubs would be responsible for supplying the players to their minor league affiliates.

This working agreement was by far the most popular method of supporting teams in the Eastern Shore League although there were two additional methods used occasionally. Sometimes the major league club would bear the entire financial responsibility of operating a minor league club, but this method was extremely rare and no documentation has been found of any Eastern Shore League team enjoying such good fortune.

A club could also be financially supported by one individual, the team operating independently of any bonds with a major league club. This was a big risk to take and on at least one occasion proved costly to an investor. Arthur Ehlers, the only man to operate an Eastern Shore League team independently (Pocomoke City in 1937 and 1938), had to devise alternative methods to meet the team's monthly salaries—including on occasion selling his personal belongings. But taking chances was nothing new to Art Ehlers, who had fought with the 29th Division in the brutal World War I battles of Meuse-Argonne in 1918. While serving his country Ehlers saw his promising baseball career end as he took a machine gun barrage in his pitching arm and had a bursting shell almost rip a leg off.

Mr. Ehlers's ESL gamble did pay off with some dividends of personal satisfaction as we'll see later when discussing the 1938 season.

The 1923 season was to be different in many aspects. Dover, Del., was selected to replace Pocomoke City, and Milford, Del., was added to the league to expand the loop to seven teams (although record books do not include Milford as a member of the 1923 Eastern Shore League). League officials anticipated additional attendance with two new teams in the league and therefore additional revenue. These expectations prompted them to allow the monthly salary limit to be raised from $1,750 to $2,000 per team for the season.

M. B. Thawley of Crisfield, Md., was elected president of the league for the 1923 season, but the memorable news came as a result of the 1922 Eastern Shore League-Blue Ridge League playoffs (Five State Championships). Word of that unique series and of a new league had filtered back to Commissioner of Baseball Kenesaw Mountain Landis and he announced he would visit the Eastern Shore during the 1923 season to investigate the new operation and its quality of play.

Even an unfortunate event just two weeks prior to Commissioner Landis's visit to the Shore failed to dampen the ESL fans' and players' excitement about his coming.

A move to eliminate a weak area (the reported lack of development of youthful players for the majors in 1922) may have stimulated a new problem and one that would flare up throughout the history of the league. The "class player" rule was initiated for the 1923 season theoretically to nurture young players with the addition of "class players" (players who had played in more than 25 games in a higher division league) on the rosters. Only three class players were allowed on each ESL team.

As previously mentioned, Milford, Del., was added to the league in '23, but dropped out of the circuit on July 5 rather than forfeit all the games they had won while using an extra class player for the brief one-month membership.

This rule and the monthly salary limit were the bases of the league's attempt to keep things fair among the various teams, although both were violated frequently throughout the history of the league. Many ESL historians attribute the failure of the league itself to these violations.

And the most notable "class player" rule violation was still 14 years away. But Delmarva baseball fans were eager for that July 19, even with the league reduced to six teams, as Judge Landis was to visit Salisbury, Md.

The commissioner arrived in Salisbury for "Landis Day" and watched with interest as the Cambridge Canners defeated the Laurel Blue Hens in a game that was regarded as the highlight of the 1923 season.

Dover went on to win the league title that year with a 51–24 record while Cambridge for the second consecutive year finished in second place just a couple of games in back of the champions.

Two 1923 ESL players were destined for the major leagues and one for the Baseball Hall of Fame. Another 1923 ESL story involved a manager who also would later be inducted into the Baseball Hall of Fame, and who that year would sign a 16-year-old farmboy who himself would become the fourth player affiliated with the Eastern Shore League to be inducted into the Baseball Hall of Fame.

Chick Tolson of Salisbury walloped 27 home runs and had 180 total bases in 1923 to lead the league in both categories and he would later perform for both the Cleveland Indians and the Chicago Cubs.

But there was also a young catcher for Dover who hit a splendid .327 (his teammate McDonald won the batting title with a .388 mark) and a modest five home runs. His name in the ESL was put on record as Frank King (to protect his amateur status), but by the time he reached the major leagues he would be known by his given name of Mickey Cochrane and of course he has since become nothing short of a baseball legend.

Yet another story of 1923 involved a man who had completed his major league career and had returned to his native Talbot County as a player/manager for the Easton Farmers. And talk about a down-on-the-farm story—Frank "Home Run" Baker had heard a number of stories about a young, robust farmboy up in Sudlersville, Md., who could reportedly hit a ball a mile. The descriptive account has always been that Baker visited this boy, named Jimmie Foxx, at his farm one day and signed the 16-year-old in the field where he had been trailing a mule and cultivator, unhesitatingly doing his chores. Foxx, of course, was destined to become a legendary baseball slugger and to this day is described by some as the greatest right-handed power hitter in baseball history.

Harry "Mac" McSherry, certainly a lesser-known person to baseball fans, was not even a player, but a writer for the *Delaware State News* and was the official scorer of the Dover team the entire 11 years the team was a member of the ESL, spanning the period 1922–48.

Much of the exposure attributed to the ESL came from Mac's correspondence. He recalled in later years the fact that Mickey Cochrane came to Dover as a second baseman, but was forced to start the season as a catcher with no previous training at the position; the rest of Cochrane's career is history.

Several pitching feats also stood out in Mac's mind. During the Five State Series of 1923 when Dover was playing Martinsburg of the Blue Ridge League, the fifth game was played at Gordy Park in Salisbury and Ira Plank, nephew of Eddie, pitched for Dover allowing the opposition but four singles. Then in 1926 Charlie Ruffing, after pitching indifferently and losing his six previous starts, went 15 innings to defeat the Salisbury Indians 1–0 on the final day of the season.

Dover defeated Martinsburg to even up the Five State rivalry—one annual series victory each.

McSherry chose Jiggs Donahue and Ray Brubaker as the outstanding Dover managers during their tenures with the Eastern Shore League.

Although Fred Lucas did not appear in the ESL in 1923, he got his professional baseball start with Martinsburg and would eventually have a short stint with the Phillies before coming to Cambridge, Md., as the 1937 Cambridge Cardinal manager. Fred was later elevated to president of the league in 1949 and never left Cambridge.

But in the winter of 1923 ESL officials were worried about the future of the league once again. They wanted to expand to an eight-team league, but were not financially able to do so. They were already in serious debt and the financial picture didn't appear to be any more promising down the road. There were serious questions as to whether the league would even operate in 1924.

Fred Lucas

But fan support and media encouragement were high as the following excerpt from the November 30, 1923, front-page article of the Cambridge *Daily Banner* suggests:

> Cambridge is again to be a member of the Eastern Shore League pennant chase in 1924. Cambridge fans are again to have the pleasure of witnessing the fastest baseball ever shown in this locality. Cambridge fans are again to have the chance of showing their sporting blood by backing the Cambridge baseball club from start to finish through a gruelling, hair-raising season as they did last year. Dorchester County fans are again to have the privilege of driving into Cambridge for the most exhilarating sport possible in the summertime.
>
> All of which means simply this—at a meeting of the baseball fans of Cambridge, held at the Chamber of Commerce rooms on Wednesday night, it was found that the sentiment was so strong for a return of organized baseball that the outgoing Directorate body of the ball club made preparations for the raising of funds with which to carry on the 1924 season, and began to take steps to clear the decks of the ship in order that the 1924 Directors might have a clear field when they go into office after next week.

Two additional decisions made at that enthusiastic 1923 meeting in Cambridge were that Herb Armstrong be hired as Canner manager for 1924 and Dr. Brice W. Goldsborough serve as chairman of the fund-raising committee. Maryland Governor Emerson C. Harrington and Chamber of Commerce President W. T. Sibbet, along with numerous other political and community leaders, also were in attendance, the article noted.

J. Harry Rew of Parksley, Va., was elected president of the league for 1924 and the season was expanded to run from May 30 to September 1.

Parksley won its second pennant in the three-year history of the league, beating out Cambridge by one game as the Canners finished in second place for the third consecutive year.

John "Jiggs" Donahue had completed a brief major league stopover with the Boston Red Sox and was managing Dover. Frank "Home Run" Baker was back at the helm of the Easton Farmers and he had his personal protege Jimmie Foxx on the roster. Charlie Fitzberger was hurling for the Parksley Spuds before heading up for a Boston Braves term. Joe Muich was under Donahue's wing at Dover and by season's end he would be with the Boston Nationals. And also at Dover was the fourth future Baseball Hall of Famer—although he did not exactly scare anyone in the ESL in 1924. Charles "Red" Ruffing posted an indifferent 4–7 won-lost record for Dover that year prior to his 20-plus years of successful mound heroics in the majors.

A former major leaguer, Ralph Mattis of Parksley, won the league batting title with a .322 clip and Zanzallari of Crisfield was the league's top slugger with 24 home runs and 185 total bases. Brown of Parksley topped the pitching victories category with 17 and teammate Hummer hurled a league-leading 221 innings.

And Congress approved a law making all Indians (including Cleveland?) citizens of the United States.

The league operated from 1925 through 1927 under difficult conditions, being continuously in the red financially and facing faltering attendance. Despite the money problems, however, there were still those, particularly the fans, who wanted the league to continue.

The Cambridge Canners finally ended their three-year stint as bridesmaids and captured the 1925 ESL pennant with a 51–38 record; the team had three future major leaguers on the squad. Pitcher Carl Fischer would later hurl for the Senators, Browns, Tigers, White Sox, Indians, and a second tour with the Senators; another hurler, Tom Glass, went from the Canners to the Philadelphia A's at the end of the '25 season; and second baseman Jimmy Jordan made it with the Brooklyn Dodgers eight years later. The top Cambridge pitcher that year, Trippe (18–5), anomalously never made it to the big time.

Additional notables of the 1925 season once again included Herb Armstrong who left the Cambridge manager position and took over the reins at Crisfield. Under Armstrong's capable tutelage was a former major leaguer and batting champion of the ESL of a year ago—Ralph Mattis—and a Crabber named Tony Rensa who would be promoted to the Detroit Tigers in 1930. Rensa, a year later, would become the focal point of another one of those forgotten Eastern Shore League circumstantial accounts. He eventually spent time with the Tigers, Phillies, Yankees, and White Sox. Bill Hohman of Easton would join the Phillies in 1927 and Phil Voyles of Parksley would head for the Boston Braves in 1929.

So despite the fact John T. Scopes was found guilty July 24 of having taught evolution in a Tennessee high school, evolution of Eastern Shore League baseball players continued.

J. Justin "Nig" Clarke was a catcher for Salisbury in 1925 after playing for four major league teams in the years before 1920.

And a homegrown Sho'man named Homer Smoot returned to the Eastern Shore and played for Salisbury that season after spending time with the Cardinals and Reds in the National League.

One more former major leaguer in the ESL in '25 was Hanson Horsey, who had toiled for the Reds in 1912, but returned to the diamond as an umpire instead of a player.

The pennant race in 1925 was the closest in the three-year history of the league and required Cambridge to dump Easton in a doubleheader on the final day of the season to edge out Parksley for the title.

St. Martin of Parksley led four batting categories that season, topped by a league-leading .363 average, 25 home runs (tied with Fitzberger of Salisbury), 78 runs scored, and 215 total bases. Another Parksley player, Firth, was far and away the mound ace with 21 victories and 131 strikeouts although Trippe of Cambridge logged the best winning percentage of .783 (18–5).

Financial problems persisted in the 1926 and 1927 seasons. These problems, however, were not the only ones; equally vexing was the fact that only one 1926 player moved up to the major leagues.

Clint Brown started the season with the Cambridge Canners, but was traded to Parksley prior to the 1927 campaign; he would later be elevated to the majors with the Cleveland Indians and the Chicago White Sox.

Two Eastern Shore League records worthy of remark were established in 1926 although later league officials would, for some unenlightened reason, ignore any records established during the 1922–27 era of the ESL.

Tony Rensa, in his second season with the Crisfield Crabbers, led the league in hitting with an unequalled .388 average and the Crisfield team won the pennant with the best winning percentage ever recorded in the ESL at .750 (63–21).

Ted Firth, for the second consecutive year, was the mainstay of the Parksley mound staff, winning over half the team's total victories. He logged the best winning percentage of .724 (21–8), recorded the most wins (21), had the most strikeouts (143), and pitched the most innings (246)— all tops in the league.

Another baseball player who came out of the 1927 Eastern Shore League was Jim Levey, who handled the shortstop position for Salisbury and was promoted to the St. Louis Browns three years later.

But it was three other young ESL players, two with Crisfield and one with Cambridge, who were looming on the horizon of major league baseball respectability.

A young catcher from Texas named Paul Richards led the Crabbers and the league in total bases and home runs in '27 with 198 and 24 respectively and of course went on as a player to Brooklyn, the New York Giants, the Philadelphia A's, and Detroit before embarking on an effective managerial career.

A young infielder teammate of Richards's was Thomas Patrick Collins out of St. Joseph's College who years later would earn reverence as a baseball talent scout marvel with the Philadelphia Phillies, and who is now better known as "Jocko" Collins. One of Jocko's acknowledged scouting treasures was Del Ennis.

While the Crabbers boasted of Richards and Collins, the Cambridge Canners were exalting an outfielder they called "Twinkletoes." It is most unfortunate that Canadian George Selkirk may best be remembered as the answer to a popular trivia question, "Who replaced Babe Ruth in right field for the New York Yankees?" For Selkirk not only held his own with the '27 Canners, but, as too many baseball supporters forget, Twinkletoes also hit over .300 five times, hit 18 or more home runs four times, and twice totaled over 100 RBIs in his nine years with the Yankees.

Parksley ran away with the 1927 Eastern Shore League pennant (60–28) and thus laid claim to being the first ESL dynasty, substantiated by capturing three pennants in the first six years of the league. To accompany that distinct honor, the Spuds put a splendid final chapter to 1927 by defeating Chambersburg in the Five State Championship and crowned themselves with glory by winning the Ned Hanlon Baseball Cup.

Paul Richards was the power batting king that final season, but Bickham of Parksley led the league in hitting at a .361 clip and collected a league-leading 119 base hits. Parksley's Brown logged the best pitching winning percentage with his 16–4 mark (.800) while Rose of Crisfield had the most wins (17) and innings pitched (237).

It was an unprecedented 1927 season: player development on the upswing and mastery over the Blue Ridge League. But a depression in the Eastern Shore League was to precede the Great Depression of the country.

Individual club and overall league financial problems continued to mount and on July 11, 1928, at the Wicomico Hotel in Salisbury, the league directors assembled and voted by a margin of four to two to disband the Eastern Shore Professional Baseball League. Lack of attendance was cited as the primary culprit for the action, which led to the first demise in the three lives of the ESL.

Harry Rew in a letter to his league treasurer attributed the end of the league to the fact "that every club was running heavily behind with no prospects of any better attendance."

So as the Eastern Shore League came in with the "Golden Age of Sports," arm-in-arm it bid goodbye; but for the ESL it was to be an extemporaneous act.

Once again without official professional-associated baseball the Eastern Shore towns from 1928 to 1936 reverted to the independent town team concept and the bitter rivalries continued at the semipro or amateur level.

There was considerable consolation in 1929 as yet another Eastern Shore native broke into the major leagues—Dick Porter debuted with the Cleveland Indians.

1922 Eastern Shore League

Team	Won	Lost	Pct.
Parksley, Va.	42	25	.627
Cambridge, Md.	37	32	.536
Crisfield, Md.	36	32	.529
Laurel, Del.	34	34	.500
Pocomoke City, Md.	29	41	.414
Salisbury, Md.	27	41	.397

Individual Pitching	IP	BB	SO	W	L	Pct.
Sheritzer, Cambridge	56	18	47	6	2	.750
Plank, Cambridge	40	27	1	3	1	.750
Klingehoffer, Parksley	173	59	158	15	5	.750
Federson, Laurel	32	8	14	3	1	.750
Godfrey, Parksley	143	21	72	11	4	.733
Knowlton, Crisfield	88	20	45	8	3	.727
Hearne, Salisbury	102	45	96	7	3	.700
Steinfelt, Laurel	83	46	25	6	4	.600
Early, Laurel	142	51	100	10	7	.588
Schroll, Cambridge	205	76	146	10	9	.526

Individual Batting	G	AB	R	H	Avg.	HR	TB
Riley, Crisfield	21	85	21	34	.400	3	61
Tagg, Crisfield	42	140	14	46	.329	1	62
Fisher, Parksley	65	256	46	83	.324	10	169
Hammen, Crisfield	63	229	39	74	.323	9	164
Early, Laurel	48	160	36	51	.318	2	91
McDonald, Pocomoke City	34	123	11	39	.317	3	99
Flowers, Cambridge	70	260	50	81	.312	14	168
Brown, Salisbury	41	143	20	44	.309	4	123
Robinson, Cambridge	31	107	12	33	.308	2	50
Hitchcock, Laurel	57	235	34	72	.307	4	144
Armstrong, Cambridge	67	213	22	53	.249	3	91

LEGEND: GB, games behind; IP, innings pitched; BB, walks issued; SO, strikeouts; W, wins; L, losses; Pct., winning percentage; CG, complete games; ERA, earned run average; G, games appeared in; AB, at bats; R, runs scored; H, hits; Avg., batting average; HR, home runs; RBI, runs batted in; TB, total bases.

1923 Eastern Shore League*

Team	Won	Lost	Pct.
Dover, Del.	51	24	.680
Cambridge, Md.	47	26	.644
Laurel, Del.	42	30	.583
Salisbury, Md.	34	39	.446
Parksley, Va.	31	45	.408
Crisfield, Md.	26	47	.356

Individual Pitching	IP	BB	SO	W	L	Pct.
Humphreys, Dover	118	27	79	12	3	.800
Hummer, Crisfield	151	49	131	11	3	.786
Fitzberger, Laurel	68	25	23	6	2	.750
Glass, Cambridge	158	8	95	12	4	.750
Plank, Dover	122	42	75	10	4	.714
Sheritzer, Cambridge	158	14	88	13	7	.650
Brown, Laurel	168	57	103	11	6	.647
Willey, Dover	156	37	81	11	6	.647
Firth, Parksley	150	41	133	11	7	.611
Stanley, Salisbury	143	29	73	10	7	.588
Phiefer, Salisbury	106	51	63	8	6	.571

Individual Batting	G	AB	R	H	Avg.	HR	TB
McDonald, Dover	65	245	60	95	.388	18	173
Kolseth, Cambridge	14	52	10	20	.385	1	30
Mattis, Parksley	65	255	43	94	.369	19	164
Tickey, Salisbury	58	201	30	74	.368	5	92
Tolson, Salisbury	57	228	57	81	.355	27	180
Phiefer, Salisbury	45	120	17	41	.341	7	68
Kraemer, Parksley	62	242	52	81	.334	15	145
King, Dover	65	245	56	79	.327	5	115
Flowers, Cambridge	66	237	50	71	.300	9	115

*Milford, Del., started the season in the ESL, but withdrew from the league July 5 rather than forfeit the games they had won because of violation of the "class player" rule.

1924 Eastern Shore League

Team	Won	Lost	Pct.
Parksley, Va.	46	34	.575
Cambridge, Md.	45	35	.563
Salisbury, Md.	44	36	.550
Crisfield, Md.	41	39	.515
Dover, Del.	41	39	.515
Easton, Md.	23	57	.281

Individual Pitching	IP	BB	SO	W	L	Pct.
Glass, Cambridge	175	23	107	14	6	.700
Miller, Crisfield-Parksley	117	44	57	9	4	.692
Brown, Parksley	211	27	128	17	8	.680
Hearne, Salisbury	214	67	175	16	8	.667
Pinto, Crisfield	114	29	94	8	4	.667
Strappe, Dover	147	32	48	10	6	.625
Muich, Dover	92	22	57	5	5	.500
Hummer, Parksley	221	57	173	12	13	.480
Trippe, Cambridge	178	45	121	11	9	.550
Ruffing, Dover	94	23	72	4	7	.364

Individual Batting	G	AB	R	H	Avg.	HR	TB
Shubert, Salisbury	40	120	23	47	.392	5	72
Kolseth, Cambridge	24	81	18	27	.333	6	51
Mattis, Parksley	73	283	53	91	.322	14	145
Sullivan, Dover	78	303	47	97	.320	16	172
Goetzel, Parksley	80	303	53	95	.314	19	174
Fitzberger, F., Salisbury	81	269	58	84	.312	10	133
Athey, Crisfield	80	315	54	95	.302	9	140
Zanzallari, Crisfield	77	302	42	90	.298	24	185
Foxx, Easton	76	260	33	77	.296	10	122
Baker, Easton	43	92	14	27	.293	5	50

1925 Eastern Shore League

Team	Won	Lost	Pct.
Cambridge, Md.	51	38	.573
Parksley, Va.	48	42	.533
Salisbury, Md.	46	44	.511
Dover, Del.	46	44	.511
Crisfield, Md.	42	48	.467
Easton, Md.	36	53	.404

Individual Pitching	IP	BB	SO	W	L	Pct.
Pope, Salisbury	75	24	50	7	1	.875
Trippe, Cambridge	192	74	129	18	5	.783
Strleckie, Crisfield	191	62	108	14	6	.700
Firth, Parksley	226	46	131	21	10	.677
Van Brunt, Dover	198	77	10	15	10	.600
Glass, Cambridge	146	28	84	10	7	.588
Fischer, Cambridge	96	47	71	7	5	.583
Miller, Parksley	232	116	128	14	14	.500
Perry, Easton	156	57	74	8	13	.381
Woods, Dover	157	37	77	6	11	.356

Individual Batting	G	AB	R	H	Avg.	HR	TB
St. Martin, Parksley	90	322	78	117	.363	25	215
Duncan, Parksley	74	287	44	101	.352	13	148
Voyles, Salisbury	84	340	68	119	.350	11	159
Aikens, Cambridge	52	183	35	63	.344	11	102
Dressen, Cambridge	89	334	65	110	.329	16	192
Fitzberger, Parksley	81	308	57	100	.321	13	146
Doherty, Dover	89	338	44	107	.317	12	167
Breslin, Crisfield	90	354	47	112	.314	9	152
Mattis, Crisfield	90	350	66	109	.311	23	197
Clarke, Salisbury	81	265	33	73	.275	3	96
Rensa, Crisfield	85	310	51	85	.274	15	146
Jordan, Cambridge	88	325	56	74	.228	8	111

1926 Eastern Shore League

Team	Won	Lost	Pct.
Crisfield, Md.	63	21	.750
Salisbury, Md.	59	29	.670
Dover, Del.	40	46	.465
Parksley, Va.	40	46	.465
Cambridge, Md.	32	54	.372
Easton, Md.	24	60	.286

Individual Pitching	IP	BB	SO	W	L	Pct.
Carlton, Easton	150	52	74	13	4	.765
Signor, Crisfield	180	46	68	11	4	.733
Firth, Parksley	246	76	143	21	8	.724
Yerkes, Dover	203	55	110	18	7	.720
Brown, C., Cambridge	154	34	62	9	6	.667
Poppen, Easton	146	46	66	11	7	.611
Smith, P., Salisbury	171	50	66	14	9	.609
Maguire, Dover	175	78	64	12	8	.600
Wood, Dover	140	47	51	10	7	.588
Pope, Salisbury	153	51	76	10	7	.588
Everham, Crisfield	215	76	81	13	15	.464

34

Individual Batting	G	AB	R	H	Avg.	HR	TB
Wilson, Salisbury	35	141	38	55	.390	6	79
Rensa, Crisfield	77	258	49	100	.388	8	144
McDougall, Parksley	86	330	59	113	.342	16	179
Sullivan, Dover	75	283	57	96	.339	12	162
Hohman, Easton	81	294	69	99	.337	15	163
Aikens, Cambridge	89	333	63	113	.336	16	188
Durning, Salisbury	81	320	54	106	.331	13	168
Fitzberger, Parksley	86	302	60	100	.331	20	174
Cather, Easton	81	315	56	104	.331	8	167
Athey, Salisbury	79	268	37	81	.302	8	125
Richards, Crisfield	58	226	35	68	.301	8	104

1927 Eastern Shore League

Team	Won	Lost	Pct.
Parksley, Va.	60	28	.681
Salisbury, Md.	48	38	.552
Crisfield, Md.	44	43	.506
Cambridge, Md.	41	47	.466
Easton, Md.	36	48	.462
Northampton, Va.	30	55	.353

Individual Pitching	IP	BB	SO	W	L	Pct.
Russell, Easton	109	32	62	9	2	.819
Brown, Parksley	194	34	77	16	4	.800
Toner, Salisbury	184	80	132	15	6	.714
Mahady, Salisbury	199	52	124	15	9	.625
Smith, Salisbury	200	38	107	13	9	.591
Everham, Crisfield	145	33	64	7	5	.584
Rose, Crisfield	237	57	94	17	13	.567
Skelton, Easton	160	65	108	10	8	.556
Trippe, Cambridge	165	59	74	11	9	.550
Anderson, Parksley	211	78	105	12	10	.546
Poppen, Easton-Parksley	185	86	65	13	11	.542

Individual Batting	G	AB	R	H	Avg.	HR	TB
Wilson, Salisbury	38	138	30	51	.369	1	69
Bickham, Parksley	88	330	68	119	.361	17	192
Selkirk, Cambridge	35	112	21	39	.349	3	51
Davidson, Parksley	69	247	44	84	.341	7	122
Pasquella, J., Crisfield	71	265	45	87	.329	12	139
Doughty, Easton	62	210	38	69	.329	13	127
Richards, Crisfield	87	332	70	107	.323	24	198
Cather, Easton-Cambridge	79	305	48	98	.322	8	156
Pasquella, D., Crisfield	87	356	53	114	.321	15	177
Lyons, Crisfield	86	344	69	110	.319	7	161

CHAPTER 4

The Eastern Shore League
Revitalized

(1937 ♦ 1941)

W HEN THE FIRST Eastern Shore League folded, some of the Shore towns—particularly Cambridge—formed leagues within each city as several local teams contested for respective city championships.

Colonel Albanus Phillips of the Phillips Packing Company and Joe Fowler of the Coca-Cola Bottling Company each sponsored teams in Cambridge. The intense competitive spirit of these two capitalists was as obvious on the baseball diamond as it was in their cunning business transactions. And in 1936—coincidentally one year prior to the reorganization of the professional Eastern Shore League—these two individuals' desire to win, as well as that of their teams, came to a head.

Perhaps in the interim since 1927, with events such as the Lindbergh kidnapping in 1932, President Roosevelt's closing of all U.S. banks in 1933, Will Rogers's death and the assassination of Senator Huey Long in 1935, competitive baseball at all levels served a need.

Cambridge's Phillips Delicious–Coca-Cola city championship series of 1936 is still a point of argument among Cambridge baseball devotees today and one is likely to hear several contradictory versions of the epic feud. But the one unwavering fact is that no less than nine professional ballplayers were ultimately involved in this "local" city championship series before the contest was settled.

The 1937 ESL Champion Salisbury Indians: back row (left to right), Jorge Comellas, John Montero, Frank Trechock, and Frank Deutsch; middle row, John Milton (treasurer), Fred Thomas, Jake Flowers (manager), John Bassler, Len Revolinsky, Joe Garlis, Joe Kohlman, Melvin Murphy (business manager); front row, Morris Fields (batboy), Bill Luzansky, Joe Reznichak, Mike Guerra, Charles Quimby, Jerry Lynn, and Edgar Leip.

Although the Coca-Cola and Phillips Delicious teams were regarded as the two best in the city and, by most accounts, on the Eastern Shore, they mysteriously did not play against each other during the regular season, but as a rule wound up as opponents in the season-ending city championship series. This was a best-of-seven-games affair, with the first game scheduled for a Sunday afternoon in early September and a single game each Sunday thereafter until one team won four games. The games were played at the Fairgrounds Park (now the location of a Little League complex) in Cambridge and well over a thousand fans were on hand for the opening game.

It was not unusual for either team to have out-of-county or, at times, out-of-state players since the true adversaries (Mr. Phillips and Mr.

Fowler) had not become successful businessmen by allowing any advantage in their best interest to escape.

By and large, though, the teams were historically composed of the best local talent available. But the 1936 series? Well, that was another story.

That particular series began, as had most of the past city championship series, with basically local lineups, and Phillips won the opener 8–2. The following Sunday Phillips ran up a two-game advantage over Coke with an 11–2 drubbing of Fowler's squad behind some fine pitching by local Ed Evans.

Coca-Cola came back to win the third game 6–3, but this game introduced some change. A Phillips player noticed that, as they were going through the pre-game warm-ups, several strange faces appeared wearing Coca-Cola uniforms. Joe Fowler had apparently opened the "ringer war" by signing a few International League players to his team in an effort to get back into the series. No one recalls the names of those initial professionals hired by Fowler, but the war was on.

What followed benefited the already more than 1,000 fans who weekly turned out for the city championship games since it was common knowledge that Colonel Phillips would surely retaliate. Rumors began spreading throughout the Shore that a baseball happening was in the making in Cambridge for the next few Sundays.

Phillips got in touch with his friend Jake Ruppert to recruit some professional ballplayers for the following Sunday and reportedly Fowler also continued to recruit for what had now become an obsession to win the 1936 Cambridge city championship.

With Phillips Delicious still leading the series two games to one, the two teams met the following Sunday. Phillips had added Max Bishop (Philadelphia Athletics) and Dick Porter (Newark and soon to be a Cleveland Indian) along with some other secret minor leaguers in retaliation for Coca-Cola's "stocking" of the previous week. Coke, however, added a few more clandestine professional players and won the fourth game 1–0 before 2,000 deliriously happy Cambridge baseball fans. The series was even at two games apiece.

By now the word had spread throughout the entire Eastern Shore that Fairgrounds Park in Cambridge was the place to be Sunday afternoon to witness a combativeness that exceeded the Hatfield-McCoy quarrel.

What had been conceived of as a local series of baseball games to decide a tiny town championship had turned into a regional exhibition of superb professional baseball, to the delight of all Delmarva—especially

40

those diehard Eastern Shore League fans who displayed undespairing allegiance to professional baseball, and who were still awaiting the return of "their" league.

The fifth game was scheduled for October 4 and a crucial game it would obviously be. Colonel Phillips decided to go one step further and added Jimmie Foxx to his lineup. The inside story was that Foxx was putting together a barnstorming team and was available for a price. Phillips reportedly paid Foxx $300 to come down from his Sudlersville home for the game, but Colonel Phillips was unaware of the fact that Foxx had decided to bring a few of his professional baseball-playing friends with him.

Jimmie Deshong of the Washington Senators pitched that October 4 and Foxx was at third base. Even though the baseball-starved Delmarva fans were not aware Foxx was to play that day some 3,000 spectators had turned out and were the beholders of one of Foxx's titanic home runs—it flew more than 400 feet away, totally out of the park at dead center field. Deshong and the Phillips team won the game 8–2 to take a 3–2 advantage in the series.

On October 11, approximately 4,000 Delmarva baseball fans crammed into Cambridge for what was to be another display of major league baseball in the little hamlet to decide the local city championship.

Phillips Delicious ended the series with a 4–2 game advantage by shutting out Coca-Cola 2–0 that memorable day and Joe Fowler probably regretted for the rest of his life recruiting a few International League players for his Coke team to get an edge. Fact was, the lineup in that final game for the "local" Phillips team included: Frankie Hayes (Athletics), Dick Porter (Newark), Jimmie Foxx (Red Sox), Jimmie Deshong (Senators), Oscar Roettger (Orioles), Henry Oana (Orioles), Billy Werber (Red Sox), Max Bishop (Athletics), and Roger Cramer (Red Sox). And rumors around the Shore persist to this day that those players were just some of the ringers drawn into the rivalry and that many others were actually involved incognito.

Whether or not the 1936 Cambridge city championships had any bearing on the Eastern Shore League's official rebirth in 1937 is subject to scrutiny, but in fact the Class D ESL did return in '37, and no single ESL game during its 1922–27 history ever drew 4,000 fans as had this final city championship game.

The country had survived the Depression, the Empire State Building had opened, Prohibition was ended in the United States, the Social

Security Act had passed through Congress, and Boulder Dam was completed—and following a nine-year absence of professional baseball in the form of an organized league on the Eastern Shore several individuals led the way for the first return of the ESL.

No one person can be credited with the idea of reviving the ESL, but the list of those involved had to include John "Dutch" Brennan, who was an umpire in the minor leagues at the time and had influential contacts with major league executives as well as some invaluable advice to give; Colonel J. Thomas Kibler, ESL president in 1937; Joe Carr, promotional director of minor league baseball, who provided the direction for the working agreement with major league baseball; Art Ehlers, who had his baseball career interrupted by the war after signing with Jack Dunn's Baltimore Orioles in 1917 and who purchased the Pocomoke City franchise as the only independently operated club in the league's history; and Harry Russell, who replaced President Kibler as the league's leader early in the 1937 season following the Colonel's heart attack. Russell would remain president until the league temporarily folded once again in 1941 at the onset of World War II.

Old ballparks had to be renovated or rebuilt; for the first time the new Eastern Shore League would be an eight-team organization; and there would be numerous switches of major league affiliations.

Salisbury, Crisfield, Cambridge, and Easton were the only four cities from the 1927 league that remained in the revival of 1937. Centreville and Federalsburg, Md., entered for the first time while Pocomoke City reentered, as did Dover, Del. The dynamo of Parksley, Va., was never again to be and the brief appearance of Northampton, Va., in 1927 was ended, so now the ESL comprised solely Maryland and Delaware teams and would continue so until the final season of 1949.

The new affiliations with the major leagues were as follows: Salisbury (Senators), Crisfield (Giants), Cambridge (Cardinals), Easton (Browns), Centreville (Red Sox), Federalsburg (Athletics), Pocomoke City (Dodgers), and Dover (International League Orioles).

The 1937 season would also be a prelude to one of the most amazing comebacks in baseball history and would focus national baseball attention on Delmarva.

League officials emphasized to team representatives that their adherence to salary limits and class player rules would be under constant, strict scrutiny since a general feeling prevailed that this would be necessary to avoid a financial disaster.

Now for the incredible incident of 1937 that, despite its controversial overtones, probably did more in a promotional sense for the ESL than any single event in the history of the league—and also ultimately bestowed a national award on the individual who precipitated it!

The Salisbury Indians (although they were a farm club for the Washington Senators, they kept their original nickname) were off to a 21–5 start that season under manager Jake Flowers. They had five future major leaguers on their team and appeared to be en route to a runaway for the pennant.

In June, however, President Kibler declared that the Salisbury team had violated the class player rule by using first baseman Bob Brady and, to teach Salisbury a lesson and to convince the rest of the league that he was sticking to his guns as far as the class player limit was concerned, he forfeited Salisbury's 21 victories, thus dropping the tribe to a 0–26 record. Not only was Amelia Earhart Putnam about to be lost forever, but it appeared as though the Indians were also out of sight.

Kibler was simply living up to his promise to keep the league clean of any violations that could jeopardize the circuit. He had often said adverse criticism and opposition were two of the penalties of leadership and he accepted them as such.

The Colonel had just imposed the most severe penalty ever on an Eastern Shore League team and soon thereafter absorbed the wrath of Clark Griffith, president of the Washington Senators, who reportedly said to Kibler, "You're doing nothing more than ruining the league."

Kibler's reply, in typical fashion, was short and to the point. "Mr. Griffith, if we can't play baseball according to the rules of the National Association, let's break up the league." No further comment was made and Mr. Griffith had nothing further to say—but the situation was now news across all the baseball world.

Kibler's integrity, never questioned by anyone closely associated with the man, would now be even more respected, since the one individual hit hardest by his judgment was Jake Flowers—a former player for Kibler at Washington College.

Flowers said later of the incident, "I was a little upset at first when the coach deprived my club of 21 games. Sure, I objected, and protested most vigorously, but I knew the old-timer meant just what he said."

The continued respect Kibler received was well deserved; perhaps his love of the game was best summed up when he remarked to a reporter in 1948, "Yes, it is true that my love for the game amounts to a religion.

Tom Kibler

Jake Flowers

I'll always be eternally grateful for baseball. I know of nothing outside of religion and education that has more salutary effect on the national character than the national pastime."

So what happened to that Salisbury club after they forfeited 21 victories? They regrouped and won 48 of their final 58 games, nipping Easton in the final week of the season for the 1937 pennant championship. And to show the baseball world more of what they could do, they continued on to take a best three out of five games in the play-off championships from Centreville. Furthermore, just to add a little icing on the cake, pitcher Joe Kohlman, a 25-game winner during the regular season, tossed a no-hitter in the final game. Kohlman, Jorge Comellas, Mike Guerra, Frank Trechock, and Jerry Lynn were later promoted to the Washington Senators.

And whatever happened to Bob Brady? The victim of circumstance also made it to the big leagues with the Boston Braves in 1946 and 1947 and today lives in Manchester, Conn.

But the imperishable events of that renaissance 1937 season don't end yet, not by a long shot.

Two Eastern Shore League pitching records were established that were never broken. Joe Kohlman's 25–1 mound feat is the best-ever winning percentage in ESL annals (.986) and Ken Raffensberger of Cambridge hurled a record 298 innings.

In addition to Kohlman's record he also led the league in complete games (23) and strikeouts (257). Lynn led the league in hitting with a .342 clip and Trechock had a league-leading 210 total bases.

Another future major leaguer out of the '37 ESL, who led the league in bases on balls issued (112), was John Wittig of Dover who apparently found the plate more accurately in time.

But the ultimate crowning glory was to be bestowed upon the man who supposedly set in motion the unequaled sequence of events. D'arcy "Jake" Flowers was named minor league Manager of the Year by *The Sporting News* for 1937!

Other notables of the 1937 season lost in the hubbub included: Fred Lucas, a former professional boxer, soccer player, and outfielder for the Philadelphia Phillies, who came to Cambridge as manager of the Cardinals and would later be president of the ESL (1949); Hal Marnie of Crisfield, who would eventually make the Phillies in 1940; Charlie Marshall (Marchiewicz), a catcher for Cambridge who would also join the Phillies in 1941; Ken Raffensberger who pitched for Cambridge and would later hurl for four major league teams from 1939 to 1954; and the two most familiar names to all baseball fans—Mickey Vernon of the Easton club and Danny Murtaugh, a rookie second baseman for Cambridge.

The 1937 Eastern Shore League survived a major scandal, and yet the league prospered more during the ensuing four years than ever before in its short history, probably directly due to the tightening-up of standards following the '37 event, as well as for the first time the true development of young ballplayers. No less than 12 Eastern Shore League players of 1937 were later promoted to the major leagues and several, such as Raffensberger, Vernon, and Murtaugh, became legitimate major league stars, although Murtaugh earned most of his fame as a manager.

Those most prosperous years (1938–41) were the pinnacle of the era which produced additional future big league stars such as Carl Furillo, Sid Gordon, Mel Parnell, Irv Hall, Gene Hermanski, Dixie Howell, Tommy Hughes, Ron Northey, Joe Ostrowski, Hugh Poland, Mel Queen, Ed Sauer, Steve Souchock, Max Surkont, Jocko Thompson, Elmer Valo, Dick West, and Jack Wallaesa, and brought forth future major league umpires Jim Boyer, Ed Sudol, and Larry Napp (who was also a player in the ESL).

The belief has always persisted that no one ever seems to be in a hurry in an Eastern Shore town. And there is some truth in that assessment, but you can be assured that a Sho' person in the act of traveling to an ESL baseball game navigated at full steam.

The abundant talent in all the teams of those years and the spicy pennant races only strengthened the baseball mania of the most dedicated as well as novice Eastern Shore League fans. There were fewer problems to deal with at the administrative level by league officials and the overall financial situation had stabilized in contrast to the problems of the 1922–27 period.

One problem persisted, however, and that was increased rowdyism. Conjecture again reverted to the cultural aspects of the location of the ESL, and the popular hypothesis was that raising hell at the ballpark was a healthy method for the farmers and watermen to release the frustrations of their arduous labor of many hours. But no one had any magical solutions to curb the problem. Delmarva was not known for metropolitan-oriented forms of art or cultural events beyond having a few cold beers and verbally abusing an umpire.

Some of the rhubarbs, scuffles, and general abuse, however, occasionally got out of hand, as can be seen in a few notable examples: Cambridge manager Joe Davis and Centreville manager Joe O'Rourke got into a heated exchange after a July 26, 1938, contest had been halted in the bottom of the eighth inning with two Cambridge base runners on and no outs. Davis and O'Rourke were discussing the possibility of resuming the game but when the pair got into fisticuffs fans poured onto the field. During the ensuing melee Francis O'Rourke, brother of the Centreville manager and club secretary, was knocked unconscious by a fan and required medical attention.

A month later (August 16, 1938) the Cambridge Cardinals defeated Easton 8–3, but umpire Clark was unable to leave the field until local police came to his aid. The Easton fans were still upset over some close calls during the contest and decided to display their hostile feelings toward Clark following the game.

Eastern Shore League fans were enthusiastically supportive of their teams and consequently felt neither the players nor the managers of their respective teams could ever be guilty of any error of judgment. During a contest between Cambridge and Dover on July 21, 1940, Cardinals manager Hugh Poland was ejected and fans immediately rose from their seats and headed for the playing field to protect Poland and take appropriate action against the umpire. Cambridge players, however, intervened on the defenseless ump's behalf and restrained the irate fans—temporarily. After the game was completed city police were called in to help the umpiring crew leave the field without being harmed by the fans who had remained to take care of some unfinished business.

And future major league umpire Jim Boyer (who officiated at ESL games during the 1937–40 era and was an ESL player years earlier) recalled the now-famous 1937 season involving the Salisbury Indians and the forfeiture of their first 21 victories. Boyer, a native of the Eastern Shore of Maryland, started his umpiring career in '37 and unfortunately had the Cambridge-Salisbury game the very night President Kibler only hours earlier had announced the Indians had to forfeit their 21 wins. Boyer recalled,

> Gordy Park was a hot spot that night. Cambridge was the visiting club. The players fought each other throughout, and those angry fans battled the umpires before and after the game. Jim O'Conner, the plate umpire, had to defend himself by swinging his mask on several guys who ganged up on him while enroute from the playing field. Yes, the

47

big leagues were a Sunday School picnic compared to that '37 Shore League season.

No doubt 1937 is the best-remembered Eastern Shore League season although the most financially stable years were 1938 through 1940. After all, the national minimum wage law was enacted in 1938.

In addition to some scandal, rowdyism, future major leaguers, and exciting pennant races, the second of three Eastern Shore League lives also produced some baseball heroes of local birth (although they did not perform in the ESL) as well as some nonplaying baseball celebrities.

Bill "Swish" Nicholson of Chestertown made his major league debut in 1936 with the Philadelphia Athletics en route to a 16-year major league career including the momentous 1943 and 1944 seasons when he led the National League in both home runs and RBIs while with the Chicago Cubs. Swish lost out in the MVP voting to Marty Marion by one vote in 1944.

Gene Corbett broke in with the Philadelphia Phillies in 1936 and stuck until 1938. He would manage the Salisbury Cardinals to the ESL pennant in 1948 and be named Manager of the Year by the Eastern Shore Sportswriters Association. At age 34, the former International League batting champion also managed to hit at a .270 clip with 83 RBIs in his player/manager role for the Redbirds.

A familiar face at ESL contests was Rex Bowen, who had signed a player contract with the Baltimore Orioles in 1934 and bounced around the minor leagues as a second baseman for a couple of years playing for the likes of Billy Southworth and Bob Rice. Rex retired as an active player in 1936, but then became a scout for the Brooklyn Dodgers after returning to his home in New Jersey. Rex and brother Joe were regulars on the Eastern Shore League scouting circuit.

Jake Flowers led the 1938 Salisbury Cardinals to their second consecutive ESL pennant, thus managing the first and only team in ESL history to win back-to-back pennants.

Sid Gordon (a future 13-year major league veteran) was the batting terror of the 1938 loop. Gordon led the league in batting (.352), triples (9), hits (145), and total bases (256) while working for the Milford Giants. Cambridge's Danny Murtaugh led the league with 13 sacrifices.

Even Gordon and Murtaugh were not anxious to hit against one Wayne Lomas of Centreville—who did *not* make it to the big time. Lomas issued 124 walks, uncorked 20 wild pitches, hit 18 batters, and lost 15 games—all tops (or lows?) in the league. Lomas was a good argument against the national minimum wage act.

Only one club franchise shift occurred in 1938 and that was the move of the Crisfield franchise to Milford, Del., where the team was accepted under the auspices of the New York Giants.

Some of the 1938 ESL graduates to the major leagues included: Irv Hall of Pocomoke City; Bob Maier of Salisbury; Al Monchak (who retired as coach of the Atlanta Braves in 1988), Mel Queen, Sr., and Dick West of Dover; and pitcher Max Surkont of Cambridge, in addition to Murtaugh, Comellas, Guerra, and Marnie.

The manager of the Easton club was Ray Powell, who had spent several years in the majors with the Detroit Tigers and Boston Braves in the early twenties.

The New York World's Fair opened in 1939 and tiny Federalsburg finally made it to the top of the Eastern Shore League as they disposed of the brief Salisbury dynasty in a big way, winning the ESL pennant by 14 games. The only disappointment for the '39 Little A's was the fact they were eliminated from the play-offs in postseason play by Dover which allowed Cambridge to capture the play-off crown.

But for all practical purposes the 1939 season belonged to the Federalsburg A's who, by the instrumentality of development, saw six of their players move on to the major leagues. And yet, ironically, the one player perhaps most responsible for the Federalsburg pennant never made it to the bigs. That '39 Federalsburg club was a hitting club, to say the least, but durable pitcher Les Hinckle was the unsung hero who held the powerful machine together.

Hinckle set three records that have stood the test of time in the ESL: he recorded 29 complete games (sharing the record with John Andre of Seaford in 1948), posted 27 victories, and struck out 309 batters. He also led the '39 league in innings pitched (283).

Another unusual aspect of that Federalsburg club, despite the fact they were notorious for the number of powerful hitters they continuously sent to the plate, is the fact not one Federalsburg batter was a league leader in any department. Collectively, however, they were awesome.

The six who graduated to the major leagues were: Ducky Detweiler (who would later return to Federalsburg as a player/ manager after his stint in the majors with the Boston Braves), Gene Hermanski (Dodgers, Cubs, and Pirates), Ron Northey (Phillies, Cardinals, Reds, Cubs, and White Sox), Joe Rullo (Athletics), Elmer Valo (Phillies, Athletics, Dodgers,

Indians, Yankees, and Senators), and Jack Wallaesa (Athletics and White Sox). The Federalsburg Athletics thus became the most prolific team of any one season in the number of graduating players sent to the major leagues.

Other 1939 Eastern Shore League teams had players who made the big time, including Joe Collins (Easton-New York Yankees), Tommy Hughes (Dover-Philadelphia Phillies), and Dixie Howell (Dover-Pittsburgh Pirates).

Cambridge for the second consecutive year, again, finished second to the pennant winners but this time it was no contest. Federalsburg etched an 83–38 record while Cambridge came in at 68–51.

A new year, a new decade, and a new development were the themes of 1940. For those of you who think player strikes are a product of recent times—you must regard nearly 50 years ago as recent times.

The Dover Orioles captured the 1940 pennant in the closest pennant race involving more than two teams in ESL annals. Are you ready for this? Milford recorded as many victories as Dover and finished third in the final official standings. Dover was 72–48 (.600), Centreville 68–48 (.586), and Milford 72–52 (.581).

It was a season of extremes. A pair of Cambridge hurlers, for example, managed to set league records they would both just as soon forget. Howard Smith dropped 17 losses (to tie Newell Valentine of Pocomoke City of the '39 season) and Steve Colosky hit 20 batters. On the brighter side of the ledger, Jorge Comellas, in his third season with Salisbury before moving up, etched a 21–10 record while working 258 innings.

A young flinger with Centreville named John "Jocko" Thompson led the league in strikeouts with 268 before being promoted to the Phillies in 1948.

Bobby Maier in his third and final season with Salisbury led the loop in base hits with 146 and a catcher from Pocomoke City named Ray Murray was the league leader in sacrifices (20) before moving on to the Cleveland Indians.

Also down in Pocomoke City was a young outfielder who turned fans on with his batting and had an arm the likes of which no one on Delmarva had seen before. He later earned the nickname "The Reading Rifle" while with the Reading, Penna., club. Carl Furillo left Pocomoke City and thereafter spent 15 years with the Brooklyn and Los Angeles Dodgers.

Other 1940 ESL graduates uptown were: Jim Gladd (Milford-New York Giants), Dick Mulligan (Federalsburg-Senators and Phillies), and

Hugh Poland (Cambridge-Giants, Braves, Phillies, and Reds). Ed Sudol would leave his Eastern Shore mask and chest protector by the Chesapeake and head for a major league career in umpiring.

The 1940 season was summed up this way by sportswriter Ed Nichols:

> The 1940 tussle stretched from one extreme to the other in matter of fan interest and color during which time the Salisbury Indians won their third playoff win in four years. The Dover Orioles captured the pennant with four games to spare.
>
> A player strike by the Salisbury club enlivened things during the final month of the season, and fans commented much about postponing a game because of "threatening weather" although the night was bright with stars shining overheard.

President Russell was ahead of time early in 1941 in being apprehensive of the storm on the horizon with war imminent and two teams (Dover and Pocomoke City) dropping out of the league, thus reducing the number of ESL teams to six. Russell acknowledged there were problems during the 1937–40 era but, compared to the financial difficulties of the 1922–27 circuit, the league had run smoothly, fan interest was higher than ever, and the money situation manageable.

Although 1941 would result in the most dismal financial season since the revitalization plan of 1937 (only two clubs showed a profit in '41) there are few who would argue that had it not been for World War II the Eastern Shore League would have continued for many more years. And many knowledgeable baseball persons contend that not only would the ESL have continued, but it would also have been fashioned into an arrangement likened to the rookie leagues of today. But Japan attacked Pearl Harbor, the United States declared war on Japan, Germany, and Italy, and the Eastern Shore League ceased to operate because of the disruption of those war years (1942–45).

So the 1941 ESL season was a lame duck interval. There was a dramatic decrease in attendance, but that may be partly attributed to the fact that Milford raced out to an early lead and won the pennant rather handily.

Manager Hal Gruber had a well-rounded baseball team with the balance of pitching and hitting that all strategists cherish. Bill Boland posted a 20–5 mound record including 20 complete games to lead the league in both departments and Chris Hayden topped the league in strikeouts with 188.

But a lanky left-hander, who would save his best pitches for a 10-year major league career with the Boston Red Sox beginning in 1947, was Milford's claim to fame at the time and his name was Mel Parnell.

Other league leaders from that Milford ball club during the final year of phase two of the Eastern Shore League were: Gordon McKinnon with a .344 batting average, 25 doubles, and 98 runs scored; Art Flesland with 157 hits; and Art Gunning with 67 RBIs. Milford, however, lost the play-off series to the Easton Yankees.

Other 1941 ESL players destined for the major leagues were: Allie Clark (Easton-Yankees, Indians, Athletics, and White Sox), Joe Murray (Easton-Athletics), Joe Ostrowski (Centreville-Browns and Yankees), and Eddie Popowski (Centreville-coach and manager of the Boston Red Sox).

No doubt the ESL suffered in more ways than one during 1941, but following that December 7 morning at Hawaii, with some 2,300 American lives lost and 19 U.S Navy ships sunk, baseball took a justifiable backseat to more significant issues.

So the league folded for a second time, thus depriving the Eastern Shore of professional baseball once again (1942 through 1945). But this time even the major leagues were understandably affected and they experienced difficult times during the war years as over 350 major league ballplayers served their country in the world turmoil.

For the young men who remained on the Eastern Shore during these years, local amateur town teams once more prevailed and all baseball fans on Delmarva hoped and prayed the war would end soon for humane reasons, but they also hoped professional baseball could and would return to the Shore.

And now that the professional Eastern Shore League had run its course for a second episode, the Delmarva individualist had also earned a reputation as a unique baseball fan. His peculiar expressions, such as "ashy" (dusty house), "cam" (calm water), and "getting up and down" (finding someone), had spread to various other areas of the country with the thousands of former ESL ballplayers who had moved on to other teams and towns or returned to their own hometowns. The country bumpkin baseball fan of the Eastern Shore was acknowledged as an astute follower of the game—even if he occasionally went beyond enthusiasm to the abuse of one of the few recreational and cultural outlets available to him.

Jesse A. Linthicum wrote in his Baltimore *Sun* column, "Sunlight on Sports," in 1939, "Baseball on the Eastern Shore is worth while. They fight for every inch over there. The fans know the game from start to finish, and they play and replay every game each night after the lights in the park are extinguished."

Delmarva's Chincoteague oysters, cherrystone clams, and broiler chickens were known across the United States. Delmarva had boasted of a mere 1,000 birds (chickens) when the ESL was formed in 1922, but by the time the league met its final demise in 1949 there were 135 million, or one-fourth the total in the entire United States. Class D minor league ballplayers spoke in awe of the Chesapeake Bay retriever as America's only native sporting dog. Oyster shucking, crab picking, dredgers, skip-jacks, and bugeyes were all revelations for those young men who came to Delmarva from all parts of America and foreign countries such as France, Canada, and Czechoslovakia. So, there can be no question as to the degree of cultural and social impact of the Delmarva area that was carried to various parts of the world by baseball players from the Eastern Shore League. And some found the area so captivating that they made Delmarva their permanent home, men such as Fred Lucas of Cambridge, Ducky Detweiler of Federalsburg, and Gene Corbett of Salisbury.

But World War II had such a devastating effect on this country and the world that officials of major league baseball were not sure themselves of just what the future of the minor leagues was to hold, and restructuring the Eastern Shore League was questionable at best.

The G.I. Bill of Rights was signed in 1944, Germany surrendered in 1945 and the Philippines were given independence by the United States in 1946 and professional baseball in the form of the Eastern Shore League returned to Delmarva.

1937 Eastern Shore League

Team	Won	Lost	Pct.
Salisbury, Md.	59	37	.615
Easton, Md.	56	41	.577
Cambridge, Md.	53	43	.552
Centreville, Md.	52	43	.547
Federalsburg, Md.	52	45	.536
Pocomoke, City, Md.	42	55	.433
Crisfield, Md.	40	57	.412
Dover, Del.	32	65	.330

Individual Pitching	IP	BB	SO	W	L	Pct.
Kohlman, Salisbury	227	55	257	25	1	.962
Comellas, Salisbury	206	66	204	22	1	.957
Rodgers, Cambridge	91	31	63	10	1	.909
Revolinsky, Salisbury	135	96	102	13	2	.867
Keene, Pocomoke City	109	27	60	8	2	.800
Raffensberger, Cambridge	298	47	183	18	6	.750
Kuntaschian, Easton	203	81	131	15	8	.652
Harris, Pocomoke City	203	91	158	15	10	.600
Radler, Easton	215	84	100	16	11	.593

	G	AB	R	H	Avg.	HR	RBI
Ogden, Centreville	210	87	72	14	12	.538	
Wittig, Dover	198	112	196	8	12	.400	
Individual Batting							
Lynn, Salisbury	93	360	96	123	.342	7	60
Trechock, Salisbury	96	388	93	131	.338	19	84
Urban, Crisfield	76	273	54	92	.337	10	62
Feinberg, Centreville	89	338	69	113	.334	15	80
Luzansky, Salisbury	96	387	100	128	.331	9	69
LeGates, Federalsburg	96	379	69	125	.330	18	81
Jackson, Cambridge	95	348	69	114	.328	12	48
Pitko, Centreville	92	363	103	119	.328	20	62
Lucas, Cambridge	29	94	7	29	.309	2	15
Murtaugh, Cambridge	94	377	71	112	.297	2	35
Guerra, Salisbury	79	314	71	93	.296	14	77
Vernon, Easton	83	300	51	86	.287	10	64
Marshall, Cambridge	88	284	40	70	.246	5	37
Marnie, Crisfield	82	302	25	72	.238	1	39
Brady, Salisbury	15	61	11	15	.246	0	7

1938 Eastern Shore League

Team	Won	Lost	Pct.
Salisbury, Md.	65	47	.580
Cambridge, Md.	61	51	.545
Milford, Del.	60	52	.536
Dover, Del.	58	54	.518
Federalsburg, Md.	56	56	.500
Easton, Md.	55	56	.495
Centreville, Md.	51	60	.459
Pocomoke City, Md.	41	71	.366

Individual Pitching	IP	BB	SO	W	L	Pct.	CG	ERA
Davis, Cambridge	196	34	144	17	5	.773	21	2.02
Yarewick, Milford	190	113	207	13	8	.619	16	2.89
Surkont, Cambridge	158	73	137	9	10	.474	15	3.13
Garner, Salisbury	172	72	120	10	7	.588	16	3.24
Bassler, Salisbury	215	53	166	17	5	.773	15	3.27
Clemence, Dover	127	29	69	12	5	.706	11	3.33
Rodgers, Cambridge	189	78	136	16	8	.667	15	3.52
Saulia, Milford	183	122	119	15	8	.652	11	4.43

Individual Batting	G	AB	R	H	Avg.	HR	RBI	TB
West, Dover	43	173	54	75	.434	22	61	161
Holbrook, Federalsburg	32	119	23	43	.361	5	28	73
Gordon, Milford	112	412	104	145	.352	25	83	256
LaPointe, Salisbury	73	300	55	103	.343	2	51	137
Schluter, Pocomoke City	77	310	69	106	.342	28	80	210
Moss, Federalsburg	17	47	7	16	.340	0	9	20
Millies, Dover	49	192	27	64	.333	1	38	85
Vandergrift, Dover	104	424	88	140	.330	13	78	206
Cielesz, Centreville	77	276	60	91	.330	12	45	160
Guerra, Salisbury	19	62	7	20	.323	0	10	31
Murtaugh, Cambridge	112	429	87	134	.312	3	52	174
Monchak, Dover	95	390	86	118	.303	10	46	183
Hall, Pocomoke City	113	469	87	136	.290	9	44	200
Maier, Salisbury	101	419	54	120	.286	7	54	166
Marnie, Centreville	112	449	81	118	.263	4	41	150
Marshall, Cambridge	92	310	40	77	.248	6	41	106

1939 Eastern Shore League

Team	Won	Lost	Pct.	Attendance*
Federalsburg, Md.	83	38	.686	27,000
Cambridge, Md.	68	51	.571	34,000
Dover, Del.	62	57	.521	23,500
Centreville, Md.	62	60	.508	21,000
Salisbury, Md.	59	59	.500	23,000
Easton, Md.	51	68	.429	32,000
Milford, Del.	49	69	.416	19,000
Pocomoke City, Md.	43	75	.364	12,000

Individual Pitching	IP	BB	SO	W	L	Pct.	CG	ERA
Hughes, Dover	80	20	85	9	0	1.000	7	1.80
Hinckle, Federalsburg	282	84	309	27	6	.818	29	2.49
McLaughlin, Cambridge	238	97	229	18	11	.621	21	2.57
Brumbeloe, Cambridge	209	108	197	20	5	.800	18	2.84
Zukowski, Salisbury	243	87	271	19	12	.613	22	2.85
Cornellas, Salisbury	78	20	77	5	5	.500	7	3.00
Brosnan, Centreville	239	128	180	14	12	.538	19	3.58

Individual Batting	G	AB	R	H	Avg.	HR	RBI	TB
Steinman, Milford	96	394	81	149	.378	17	94	247
Valo, Federalsburg	34	115	28	43	.374	3	19	65
Holbrook, Federalsburg	98	305	65	110	.361	20	81	191
Northey, Federalsburg	79	321	85	110	.343	23	70	214
Kolberg, Federalsburg	122	472	111	160	.339	21	121	261
Monchak, Dover	104	389	88	131	.337	15	73	210
Hall, Pocomoke City	61	255	45	86	.337	9	39	127
Walsh, Centreville	122	487	94	163	.335	28	129	292
McGonegle, Milford	117	452	87	148	.327	24	99	248
Maier, Salisbury	119	470	77	153	.326	11	79	225
Schluter, Dover	116	429	92	139	.324	29	100	258
Russo, Salisbury	101	388	61	121	.312	9	67	176
Howell, Dover	86	298	53	93	.312	8	54	141
Vergnani, Dover	121	473	85	147	.311	18	76	236
Detweiler, Federalsburg	98	342	74	100	.292	10	49	151
Souchock, Easton	65	241	35	62	.257	8	36	118
Rullo, Federalsburg	112	469	91	115	.245	9	39	173
Consoli, Cambridge	30	123	19	30	.244	1	18	39
Wallaesa, Federalsburg	40	131	10	27	.206	1	22	35
Hermanski, Federalsburg	10	46	13	9	.196	0	7	18

*Data from *The Sporting News*, November 2, 1939, page 5.

59

1940 Eastern Shore League

Team	Won	Lost	Pct.
Dover, Del.	72	48	.600
Centreville, Md.	68	48	.586
Milford, Del.	72	52	.581
Salisbury, Md.	65	58	.528
Federalsburg, Md.	57	67	.460
Cambridge, Md.	52	67	.437
Easton, Md.	48	69	.410
Pocomoke City, Md.	50	75	.400

Individual Pitching	IP	BB	SO	W	L	Pct.	CG	ERA
Thompson, Centreville	208	74	268	18	5	.783	21	1.56
Carretta, Milford	227	87	218	14	10	.583	18	1.82
Comellas, Salisbury	258	60	203	21	10	.677	22	2.20
Johnson, Dover	113	50	95	11	2	.846	11	2.23
Mulligan, Federalsburg	196	55	164	16	8	.667	20	2.25
Jaust, Centreville-Dover	177	35	92	16	4	.800	17	2.44
Reisberg, Federalsburg	213	75	129	16	9	.640	19	2.45
Colosky, Cambridge	218	100	167	14	10	.583	21	2.68
DeMartini, Milford	194	50	154	16	6	.727	16	2.74
Hogan, Dover	208	53	146	13	11	.542	20	3.03

	G	AB	R	H	Avg.	HR	RBI	TB
Kallenberg, Milford	194	71	125	16	7	.696	20	3.20
Murray, J., Easton	128	71	93	6	14	.300	10	3.52
Individual Batting								
Rice, Federalsburg	97	342	63	124	.363	7	54	169
Weiss, Pocomoke City	99	385	81	137	.356	17	60	226
Clark, Dover	102	331	52	116	.350	9	66	169
Olt, Cambridge	116	435	77	140	.322	1	46	174
Kobesky, Salisbury	75	257	49	82	.319	18	58	154
Furillo, Pocomoke City	71	235	36	75	.319	9	39	123
Jaeger, Milford	110	366	62	116	.317	9	75	186
Swoboda, Dover	117	437	87	136	.311	0	75	171
Poland, Cambridge	88	306	44	95	.310	7	56	140
Hermanski, Federalsburg-Pocomoke City	121	431	79	133	.309	11	54	194
Maier, Salisbury	124	511	70	146	.286	1	61	168
Sauer, Easton	49	179	26	50	.279	2	25	73
Harrigan, Milford	113	444	72	117	.264	12	66	186
Murray, R., Pocomoke City	90	308	38	81	.263	2	39	100
Gladd, Milford	84	262	32	57	.218	9	41	95
Rullo, Federalsburg	115	415	62	88	.212	5	33	122

1941 Eastern Shore League

Team	Won	Lost	Pct.
Milford, Del.	66	41	.611
Cambridge, Md.	61	45	.575
Easton, Md.	57	53	.518
Centreville, Md.	54	52	.509
Salisbury, Md.	51	59	.464
Federalsburg, Md.	35	73	.324

Individual Pitching	IP	BB	SO	W	L	Pct.	CG	ERA
Ostrowski, Centreville	126	29	74	10	4	.714	12	1.71
Rundus, Cambridge	230	66	159	17	13	.567	19	1.80
Johnson, Cambridge	163	44	164	12	6	.667	14	2.10
Boland, Milford	205	60	187	20	5	.800	20	2.15
Holmes, Easton	185	63	139	13	7	.650	13	2.29
Murray, H., Salisbury	160	79	71	10	12	.455	14	2.31
Curran, Cambridge	152	64	96	11	5	.688	14	2.31
Summers, Cambridge	205	62	124	15	8	.652	17	2.50
Murray, J., Easton	144	61	140	13	8	.619	9	3.13
Hayden, Milford	219	88	188	15	8	.652	17	3.53
Parnell, Centreville	48	16	29	4	4	.500	4	4.13

Individual Batting	G	AB	R	H	Avg.	HR	RBI	TB
McKinnon, Milford	106	424	98	146	.344	10	60	201
Forwood, Federalsburg	99	387	44	131	.339	3	66	175
Flesland, Milford	110	474	80	157	.331	2	31	189
Gunning, Milford	94	365	54	120	.329	6	67	160
Koval, Cambridge	105	371	94	121	.326	16	66	209
Tyler, Cambridge	80	289	45	94	.325	2	37	117
Clark, Easton	70	268	38	87	.325	7	47	137
Price, Milford	94	365	66	115	.315	8	66	173
Gruber, Milford	92	325	57	100	.308	4	48	129
Maier, Salisbury	110	442	56	126	.285	4	48	155

CAMBRIDGE DODGERS

BASEBALL CLUB, Inc.
CAMBRIDGE, MARYLAND

SUPPORT YOUR CAMBRIDGE BALL CLUBS:
DODGERS—MERCHANTS—AMERICAN LEGION

Eastern Shore League

GOOD LUCK DODGERS

CAMBRIDGE MOTOR SALES, Inc.
FRED ENSOR, Mgr.

Sales  Service

The cover of a Cambridge Dodgers home game program.

CHAPTER 5

The Third and Final Eastern Shore League

(1946 ♦ 1949)

*T*HE ENTHUSIASM of the ESL fan had never been questioned—although at times it was described as being somewhat unrestrained—during the first two tenures of the league and this was a viable, marketable asset for those who were in the act of reinstating the ESL for the third time in 1946.

Ballparks had to be renovated or new ones built and there was reluctance on the part of major league owners to reestablish minor leagues that had not survived World War II. Cutbacks were in order at all levels of professional baseball, but especially at the Class D level.

One must remember, however, that a true Eastern Shore person is persistent, if not stubborn, and when he or she is out to hook a fish—or, as in this case, to bring professional baseball back to the Shore—they'll usually find a way to do it. And believe it or not it was a fish story that brought results in another rebirth of the ESL.

John Perry of Centreville, Dr. W. K. Knotts of Federalsburg, Dr. Walter Grier of Milford, and Fred Lucas of Cambridge were foremost among those trying to revive the ESL this time. Harry Russell of Easton would have undoubtedly assumed an active role in this project but he was still on active duty with the Air Force.

Fred "Fritz" Lucas, a former Philadelphia Philly who had been employed by the Brooklyn Dodgers since 1937 when he was sent to Cambridge to manage the Class D club, was perhaps the most influential person in the redevelopment of the league and he used some good ole Eastern Shore improvisation to contrive the end result. Fred had learned the ways of a Sho'person during the nine years he had lived in Cambridge although he was originally from the Philadelphia area.

The Cambridge Canners (1922–27) and the Cambridge Cardinals (1937–41) were, along with the Salisbury Indians, far and away the most successful franchises of the two previous Eastern Shore Leagues. And both cities still had fair ballparks for their day. But by 1946 the major league operators wanted parks far superior to those that had been utilized in the two previous ventures of the ESL.

Lucas was well aware of the intricate workings of both major and minor league operations from the front office to the playing field. He, along with additional supporters of the reorganization of the league, realized that if just one major league club would provide some financial assistance in either renovating old parks or building new parks, the other major league teams would probably "follow the leader" and add their support, and thus the league might resume.

Obtaining that first commitment, however, would be a monumental task and Fritz Lucas was the man most qualified to shoulder such responsibility.

Fred journeyed to Brooklyn on several occasions during the winter of 1945 to drive a bargain with Branch Rickey on the reorganization of the ESL and specifically to have the Dodgers support a minor league club in Cambridge. The amiable relationship between Lucas and Rickey was well known throughout baseball circles and on one occasion Fred finally convinced Rickey to vacate New York and set sail on the Choptank River for some fishing. The baseball pair joined Milford Elliott on his boat and during the cruise hooked in excess of 100 hardheads. Brimming with pride, the owner of the Brooklyn Dodgers stuffed his catch in a borrowed suitcase and hauled the scented delight back to his Brooklyn home just to make sure the city slickers would believe his fish story.

Cambridge and the Eastern Shore had no doubt made an impression on Mr. Rickey from at least one standpoint, and a few months later he returned at Mr. Lucas's request to go duck hunting in the lower portion of Dorchester County. Lucas again made all the necessary arrangements and had his friend Adrian Hansen serve as a guide for Rickey and his party. Lucas, of course, fully intended to mix some business with pleasure on this particular outing.

And once again, as was and is usually the case with hunting and fishing on the Eastern Shore of Maryland, the intrepid hunters were most successful in their quest. Mr. Rickey was so impressed that he even informed Guide Hansen the next time the Dodgers won the pennant he would have World Series tickets ready and waiting for him.

Two years later, in 1947, Brooklyn took the pennant and Mr. Hansen was the recipient of the World Series tickets as promised and also had hotel reservations—all at the expense of Branch Rickey.

And Fred Lucas's scheme was crowned with success, for Mr. Rickey had committed to a "new" $60,000 Dodger Park in Cambridge for the 1946 season. The assumption that the other league supporters would fall in line proved accurate, as soon thereafter several major league owners followed suit with commitments for renovations of parks in other towns.

Now that the monumental hurdle had been cleared it was time for Lucas and interested Eastern Shore baseball persons to forge ahead full steam to reorganize the Eastern Shore League for the upcoming 1946 season.

Colonel Kibler was once again elected president of the league and the number of teams was again elevated to eight. Several franchise shifts occurred, however, in addition to the Dodgers assuming responsibility in Cambridge. The St. Louis Cardinals took over at Salisbury. Dover was backed by the Philadelphia Phillies. Milford became the property of the Boston Red Sox. And the Seaford Eagles had a working agreement with the New York Giants. Federalsburg remained with the Athletics as did Easton with the Yankees, and Centreville joined up with the Orioles of the International League.

The Centreville club made its presence known quickly that 1946 season as it became the only ESL team, during the final seven years of operation of the league, to win both the pennant and the play-offs in the same year. The Orioles, managed by Jimmy McLeod, clinched the pennant in early August with an 18-game lead over runner-up Milford. The Birds then went on to wipe out both Dover and Milford in the play-off competition.

Jimmy Stevens led the league in stolen bases (80) and set a league record in runs scored (132) for the Orioles that year.

Curiously, Centreville was one of a very few teams in the '46 ESL which did not have a future major league player on its roster, although

EASTERN SHORE BASEBALL LEAGUE

the president and general manager of the team was Jack Dunn, who later served in most front office positions of the Baltimore Orioles when they came over from St. Louis in 1954.

Fred Pacitto and Nick Malfara were the top hitters for the ESL Orioles, each swatting .342 for the year. Malfara, however, showed slightly more power in the overall statistics of the pair, hitting 10 home runs with 99 RBIs. Heuser posted a 6–0 mound record and recorded a 1.10 ERA while appearing in only seven games for the Centreville club. Coulling was 17–8 and Cave ended the season with a 14–8 mound record.

Players from the 1946 ESL destined for the major leagues were: Joe Becker (Seaford-Indians), Steve Bilko (Salisbury-Cardinals, Cubs, Reds, Dodgers, Tigers, and Dodgers again), Lew Krausse, Sr. (Federalsburg-Athletics), Duke Markell (Seaford-Browns), Tom Poholsky (Milford-Cardinals and Cubs), and Chris Van Cuyk (Cambridge- Dodgers).

Posting a forgettable 8–13 pitching record that year was an 18-year-old Nebraska native named Carroll Beringer on the Cambridge Dodger staff who would spend over 30 years with the Dodger organization as player, pitching coach, and bull pen coach.

The 1947 ESL season would turn around not only Carroll Beringer's baseball career but also the Cambridge Dodger franchise and the Eastern Shore League.

Jackie Robinson joined the Brooklyn Dodgers April 11 to make major league history and the Cambridge Dodgers won their second—and last—ESL pennant, while setting a professional baseball winning percentage record for that season. The league as a whole flourished with numerous future major leaguers, a smattering of former major leaguers, and, most importantly, long-to-be-respected baseball authorities in various administrative and front office positions.

Tom Kibler was elected president, secretary, and treasurer once again; and he had a veteran baseball staff which included Vice-president Dr. Walter L. Grier and Directors Fred Lucas, John Strickland, Ray Guthrie, J. Howard Anthony, Dr. J. Edwin Dunn, E. Roscoe Calloway, Lawrence Walmsley, and Dr. W. K. Knotts. Hanson Horsey was named umpire-in-chief.

And added to this worthy staff were four former major league players who managed in the ESL that year: Roy Nichols (Giants '44) at Cambridge, Joe Antilock (Phillies '44) at Easton, Elmer "Pep" Rambert (Pirates '39–40) at Federalsburg, Walt Millies (Dodgers, Senators, and Phillies) at Milford, and a few accomplished baseball people such as Hall

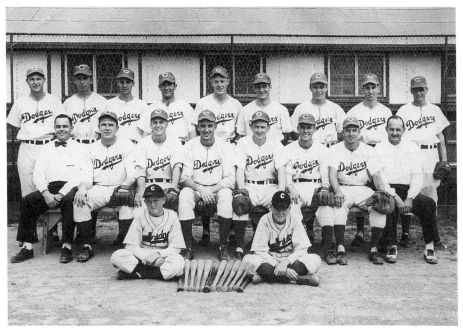

The 1947 ESL champion Cambridge Dodgers: back row (left to right), Roy Nichols (manager), Carroll Beringer, Ralph Reimer, Danny Dever, Bob Stramm, Dennis Reeder, Wheaty Sperato, Bill Ripken, Lou Magee; front row, Charlie Slacum (business manager), Mike Quill, Phil Lewindowski, Chris Van Cuyk, Merrill McDonald, Joe Umholtz, Charlie Tim Thompson, Fred Lucas (ESL president); seated in front, Henry Taitt and Joe McAllister (batboys).

of Famers Herbert J. Pennock (vice-president of the Dover club), Connie Mack (president of the Federalsburg club), and son Earle Mack (vice-president, Federalsburg).

Rehoboth Beach, Del., had replaced the 1946 champion Centreville team in the league, but 1947 was to be a Dodger year for Cambridge from start to finish.

Cambridge had built a 16-game lead by early August after opening a 15-5 start in their first 20 contests. They completed the onslaught with a final 91–34 (.728) won-lost record—the best in professional baseball in 1947. The 91 victories set an Eastern Shore League record which was never broken.

The Dodgers also topped the league in attendance that season, drawing 62,118 spectators. They then inked a single game play-off attendance mark when 3,692 paid admissions (3,761 total) squeezed into

Dodger Park (seating capacity 2,267) on September 15 at a semifinal play-off contest against Dover; all went home ecstatic as pitcher Chris Van Cuyk shut out the Phillies 3–0.

The dream season ended shortly thereafter, however, as the Dodgers were eliminated by a stubborn Seaford Eagle club four games to three in the play-off finals with 16-game winner Dean Crooks tossing a one-hitter to beat Beringer and the Dodgers 6–0 in the final game of the season.

The Dodgers had made a jump from seventh to all-powerful champions in a single season primarily through some shrewd signings on the part of Branch Rickey and Fred Lucas and the able leadership of Roy Nichols.

Van Cuyk set an ESL record for shutouts with nine and Charley "Tim" Thompson inked a new league mark for triples with 14.

Van Cuyk and Beringer (he forgot that '46 season and came back with a vengeance) were the top hurlers for the 1947 Dodgers during that fruitful season with 25–2 (1.94 ERA) and 22–6 (2.55 ERA) records respectively and Mike Quill etched an 18–3 mark.

It was an exciting and, to say the least, out-of-the-ordinary season, with the only visible guarantee being that the Dodgers would win the pennant.

Gordon McKinnon opened the season as manager of the new Rehoboth Beach team, but was released during the season and joined Seaford, where he helped the Eagles to a second-place finish in the regular season and upset the Dodgers in the play-off series. McKinnon hit .344 on the season with 90 RBIs.

The '47 league batting champion was player/manager Pep Rambert of Federalsburg who swatted .376 on the year beating out teammate Robert "Ducky" Detweiler and three Cambridge Dodgers. Cambridge player/manager Roy Nichols hit .355 followed by Detweiler (.352), Tim Thompson (.349), Bill Ripken (.347), and still another Dodger, Bob Stramm, who hit a healthy .340 average.

Cambridge players for obvious reasons dominated the league leaders in both pitching and hitting that year although Detweiler, who had his original start in the ESL in 1939, was to be named Most Valuable Player.

Detweiler still holds a special place in the hearts of most Delmarva baseball fans, one reason being he has never left Federalsburg since he came to the little hamlet with the ESL team from his Trumbauersville,

Penna., home as a teenager. Ducky had one of those hard-luck stories that everyone seems to identify with. After his initiation at Federalsburg in '39 he worked his way to the major leagues with the Boston Braves in 1942. At the prime age of 23 he made his major league debut under the watchful eye of one Casey Stengel. The gutty former ESLer hit the first pitch ever thrown to him in the big leagues for a single and his overall debut resulted in a 3 for 7 performance in a doubleheader. Ducky appeared in 12 games that year as a rookie hitting .318 and was a sure-bet major league star of the future.

But, like thousands of other young men of the time, he was drafted into the military and the following years were spent at war. He appeared in one game for the Braves in 1946 going 0 for 1, leaving his major league career batting average at .311 while performing in 12 games at third base.

Detweiler could have given up the game and entered another profession now that the war had taken its toll on his abilities. But Robert Sterling Detweiler would have none of that nonsense. He was sent back to Federalsburg where he literally terrorized ESL pitchers for the next three years.

He earned his MVP award in 1947 based on his league-leading 29 home runs, 133 RBIs, and 269 total bases. And had a 19-year-old from Royal Oak, Mich., not come along during the 1948 Eastern Shore League season, Ducky would have absolutely gone down in ESL history as the greatest batting performer ever.

He still has to be considered the finest consistent ESL hitter, taking into account his accomplishments during his three-year playing career (1947–49). Detweiler was also player/manager of the Federalsburg A's for the 1948 and 1949 seasons and later was a high school and college referee/umpire for some 30 years on the Eastern Shore following the ESL's final season in 1949.

But back to some other 1947 league leaders (and there were some other than Ducky): Duke Makowsky (who changed his name to Markell when he reached the major leagues with the Browns) of Seaford and Chris Van Cuyk of Cambridge topped the league in complete games for pitchers with 24 each. Van Cuyk also topped the league in strikeouts (247) and ERA (1.94) while Makowsky led the league in innings pitched (249).

Cambridge's player/manager Nichols led the league in doubles (35) while his Dodger teammates dominated the rest of the batting statistics left over by Detweiler. Charley Tim Thompson and Bob Stramm each collected 162 hits and Stramm led the league in runs scored with 129. Don Petchow of Cambridge and Charles Havelka of Federalsburg shared the questionable honor of being hit by the pitcher most with each being struck 12 times.

Those of the ESL class of '47 who headed for the major leagues included: John Andre (Seaford-Cubs), Ray Jablonski (Milford-Cardinals, Reds, Giants, and A's), Markell-Makowsky (Seaford-Browns), Herb Moford (Salisbury-Cardinals, Tigers, Red Sox, and Mets), Joe Muir (Rehoboth Beach-Pirates), Nick Testa (Seaford-Giants), Tim Thompson (Cambridge-Dodgers, Athletics, and Tigers), Don Thompson (Milford-Braves and Dodgers), Van Cuyk (Cambridge-Dodgers), and Spider Wilhelm (Federalsburg-Athletics).

The Kinsey report on sexuality in the human male was published in 1948, but it received Tom Thumb reviews on the Eastern Shore compared to the workmanship of the Salisbury Cardinals as a team and that of a Milford first baseman as an individual.

Dallas Culver of Seaford was elected president of the league for the 1948 season and, as '47 was the year of the Cambridge Dodgers, '48 was to be the year of the Salisbury Cardinals from a team standpoint. But a Milford first baseman, whose story is told later, would win the respect of Eastern Shore League fans, who came to hold him in their hearts, entwined with their own Ducky Detweiler.

Last in '47 and first in '48 was the one-year success story of the Salisbury Redbirds—almost a duplicate feat of the 1946–47 Cambridge Dodger story.

The Cardinals thus tied with Parksley as the only two Eastern Shore League teams to capture three pennants, but the Redbirds had a 10-year wait to notch that third title. As Cambridge had the previous year, however, they fell victim in the play-off series, being eliminated by the Easton Yankees. The Milford Red Sox, with their awesome power display, progressed to win the play-off championship.

And for the second consecutive year the Eastern Shore League champion posted the highest winning percentage in professional baseball, thus earning the Shore loop the popular title "the fastest Class D League in the country."

For some inexplicable reason, overall league attendance dropped 106,537 in 1948 from the record 374,479 fans of the previous year. One would be hard pressed to attribute the decline to the runaway pennant

This photo taken from center field of old Dodger Park in Cambridge in 1947 was the scene of a record crowd (3,761) attending a play-off game between Cambridge and Seaford. The park is now J. Edward Walter Memorial Park.

efforts of the Salisbury club since the Cambridge club led from start to finish during the 1947 record-setting attendance year.

There were no franchise shifts, but rumors persisted that working agreements with the major leagues would be difficult to obtain in the future if a solution to the attendance problem was not forthcoming. The fact of the league towns' limited population base was certainly nothing new and did not seem to have affected the numbers of fans attending games a year earlier, but lack of local monetary support to complement the working agreements may have been discouraging to the parent teams—especially in the area of upkeep of the ballparks.

The Salisbury team clinched the pennant on August 28 with an 11-game advantage for player/manager Gene Corbett (another who came to the Shore via the ESL and continues to make it his home). And when the dust settled, the Cardinals had stretched an 89–32 (.736) record to better the Cambridge Dodgers' .728 mark set a year earlier. Ironically, the second-best winning percentage in baseball that 1948 season was achieved by West Frankfort, Ill., of the Illinois State League which was managed by Harold Contini (the 1946–47 manager of Salisbury). West Frankfort captured its league pennant with a .708 percentage.

Cambridge's 91 victories of 1947, however, still stand as the most ever in any one season in ESL history. And the league record .750 winning percentage of the 1926 Crisfield Crabbers remained intact.

The only time during the 1948 season the Salisbury team felt any concern was in mid-July when they dropped four in a row (their longest losing streak for the season) and allowed Milford to creep within six and a half games of the lead. The Cardinals broke out of the slump, however, and rattled off nine straight victories and by August 1 had a comfortable 10 1/2 game advantage.

Pitching and defense were the hallmarks of Corbett's squad, as only one player hit over .300 on the season and the Redbirds were primarily powerless at the plate. They led the league in defense and had three of the top pitchers in the league.

Corbett's strategy, based on the type of players he had to work with, was to force the opposing team to lose a game rather than attempting to win a game with the bat. And it was a piece of managerial genius when you consider that every member of the 1948 Salisbury team, with the exception of four, had been molded together at spring training in Albany, Ga. During the spring training exhibition games the Cardinals posted a 12–3 record against stiff opposition from Class C and B rivals.

They would hit and run, pull off delayed steals, squeeze bunts, and take the extra base; and they utilized the sacrifice bunt 113 times in 121 games.

They had the most dependable infield in the league to go along with a formidable mound staff. Corbett, a former major leaguer, was at first base, Don Davis at second, Whitey Koppenhaver at shortstop, and Mike Rivera at third. Rivera led the Redbirds in hitting with a .323 average, had 83 RBIs, and scored 72 runs.

But the Salisbury pitching staff ranked one-two-three in the final league statistical categories with Ed Black, Carl Wollgast, and Herb Moford. Black had the best ERA in the league with a 2.23 mark while posting a 16–5 record. Wollgast came in with a 2.26 ERA and a 17–6 mound ledger, while Moford recorded an outstanding 20–4 slate with a 2.39 ERA.

No less than ten new Eastern Shore League records were etched that 1948 season with one being Whitey Koppenhaver's 22 sacrifices for Salisbury.

Don Maxa of Easton hit .382 which the ESL Sportswriters Association viewed as a new record, ignoring McDonald's (Dover, 1923) and Tony Rensa's (Crisfield, 1926) .388 marks. Ray Jablonski of Milford rapped out 172 hits, Don Nicholas of Cambridge swiped 82 bases, and pitcher John Andre of Seaford tied two league marks: complete games (29 to tie Les Hinckle) and hits allowed (272 to tie Lew Krausse, Sr.).

But a lesson was learned that 1948 season and it has been repeated at all levels of baseball since. Pitching and defense are most important over a long season, but when it comes to a short series the big bats will more often than not take over.

Hence Milford won the play-off championship, and now, to illustrate the big bat theory, we'll introduce you to the young Milford Red Sox first baseman we've mentioned on two occasions.

Norm Zauchin of Milford literally ripped the Eastern Shore League apart with his bat that year before joining the parent Boston team two years later. Zauchin was at the time the property of Louisville of the American Association League and it was obviously just a matter of time before he would hit the major leagues.

In 1948 Norm Zauchin established the following ESL batting records: doubles (44), home runs (33), RBIs (138), and total bases (323). In 120 games he hit .353 (third best in the league) and scored 126 runs.

And who was this enormous (6'4", 220 lbs.) kid anyway? Ducky Detweiler wasn't about to let Zauchin bump him from his eminent standing among Eastern Shore League fans, and kept himself in the spotlight with a nearly matching performance by hitting .341 with 21 home runs, 95 RBIs, 219 total bases, and 86 runs scored.

Zauchin was not totally a one-man show for his club although he made a good try of it. Charlie Price of Milford tied Tommy Tanner of Rehoboth Beach for the league lead in triples with 12 each.

On the pitching side of the ledger John Andre of Seaford was more of a one-man show than Zauchin was for the batters. Andre topped the league in wins (21), complete games (29), strikeouts (228), innings pitched (263), walks issued (148), wild pitches (14), hit batsmen (18), and hits allowed (272), and managed an overall 21–12 won-lost record for the Eagles. Andre thus became the most prolific provider of season statistics in ESL history, topping eight different categories.

Cambridge finished fourth in 1948, but gained respectability when they rose from dead last on Decoration Day (10 games out of fourth place) to their final fourth place in the standings.

Stew Hofferth took over as player/manager for Bob Vickery and was credited with turning the Cambridge club around. With Hofferth at the helm and playing well (.335 batting average) the Dodgers won 21 of 32 games.

There were other managerial changes in 1948: Harry "Socks" Seibold replaced Bobby Westfall at Seaford and Grover "Worm" Wershing took over for Guy Glaser at Dover.

Despite the storm warnings for the future of the Eastern Shore League that appeared in 1948 the league still produced its share of future major leaguers as well as more than its share of league records. Headed for the big leagues were: John Andre (Seaford-Cubs), Hal Bevan (Rehoboth Beach-Red Sox, Athletics, and Reds), Ray Jablonski (Milford-Cardinals, Reds, Giants, and Athletics), Frank Malzone (Milford-Red Sox and Angels), Bob Micelotta (Dover-Phillies), Herb Moford (Salisbury-Cardinals, Tigers, Red Sox, and Mets), Jack Sanford (Dover-Phillies, Giants, Angels, and Athletics), Gale Wade (Cambridge-Cubs), and of course Norm Zauchin (Milford-Red Sox and Senators).

It had become obvious to most of the Eastern Shore League officials in 1948 that the major league baseball organizations were contemplating ceasing financial support of the ESL and that 1949 could very well be the last year of existence for the grand old league.

Fred Lucas, associated with the league since 1937, was elected president and W. Ross Collins of Seaford was named vice-president.

Milford and Dover pulled out of the league in 1949, leaving the loop with just six teams once again. Attendance dropped another 55,000 during the '49 season and most all Shore baseball fans knew the end was near.

Easton made the most of that final season, winning its first and only pennant in 13 years of association with the ESL. Jack Farmer led his Yankee farm club to a title four and a half games ahead of Federalsburg.

Wally Burnette fashioned a 13-6 mound record for Easton with a 2.77 ERA, and the Yankees were led at the plate by Gordon Bragg with a .362 average and by Andy Anderson with a .310 batting clip.

Bill Sisler, manager of the Rehoboth Beach club, worked his renowned family baseball magic to take the play-off championship series and bring a final curtain down on professional baseball on Delmarva. Perhaps it was an omen that Rehoboth Beach did not carry the traditional major league name tag of their affiliate—the Pirates had withdrawn support and the Rehoboth Beach team was known as the Sea Hawks.

The only league record set in 1949 was an inconspicuous one as pitcher A. Schultz of Salisbury issued 165 bases on balls.

The league leader in losses was a youngster named Stu Miller of Salisbury who dropped 13 contests, but who would get his career in gear in 1950.

By December 1949 it was almost a certainty the Eastern Shore League was soon to be disbanded. Fred Lucas headed a group of interested Delmarva baseball enthusiasts who would do everything possible to save the league that had meant so much to so many for 15 years of operation. Meetings were scheduled all over the Shore. New ideas. Expansion to the western shore. Fewer games. Shorter seasons. Fewer players on rosters. Lower salaries. Lucas favored some of the new ideas and even presented many himself. (It was no coincidence that when the rookie leagues were formed in the fifties they had a very basic and obvious parallel to the suggested format of the never-to-be 1950 Eastern Shore League.)

But 1949 was not to leave the Eastern Shore with empty baseball memories. The '49 ESL, despite having a dismal season by most accounts, produced several future major league players: Wally Burnette (Easton-Athletics), Bert Hamric (Cambridge-Dodgers and Orioles), Stu Miller (Salisbury-Cardinals, Phillies, Giants, Orioles, and Braves), Joe Pignatano (Cambridge-Dodgers, Athletics, Giants, and Mets), and Don Zimmer (Cambridge-Dodgers, Cubs, Mets, Reds, Dodgers, and Senators). In 1988 Pignatano was coaching with the Atlanta Braves and Zimmer was manager of the Chicago Cubs. And there are literally dozens more former ESLers scouting for major league clubs today or involved in various other aspects of the game of baseball.

The 1949 season also produced one more professional baseball player who found Delmarva so enchanting that he remained here for the rest of his life. Buck Etchison had a brief stint with the Boston Braves (1943–44) before eventually being assigned to Federalsburg in 1949. He like others such as Detweiler, Lucas, Corbett, Baker, Smoot, and Betts, chose either to return to their Eastern Shore homeland or to make Delmarva their home and become adopted sons and true Sho' persons.

The Class D professional Eastern Shore League gave up the ghost for the third and final (as of this writing) time in 1949, but an Eastern Shore League and a Central Shore League continued on and still exist today much akin to the original amateur or semipro town teams of the early 1900s.

In 1951 the Cambridge Baseball Club, after completing an 18–12 regular season record, took on an all-star team from the professional Georgia-Florida League and drubbed the visitors 10–4 to jog some memories of local baseball capabilities with one Robert "Ducky" Detweiler leading the way for the local nine.

In 1952 the International League Orioles came to Cambridge's American Legion Park (old Dodger Park) to do some preseason training with a few locals helping out.

When anyone checked the final batting averages of the 1953 major league there was no need to remind a Delmarva person that both batting champions (Mickey Vernon and Carl Furillo) were former Eastern Shore League players. And since Fred Lucas didn't have a team to manage or a league to preside over he simply bought a block of 200 Baltimore Oriole tickets so that Cambridge youngsters could witness professional baseball. Art Ehlers was the new Orioles general manager that year. Warren "Sheriff" Robinson of Cambridge ended his playing career and started his coaching career, which would eventually carry him to the New York Mets.

Bona fide professional baseball did indeed return to old Dodger Park in 1955 as Al Kaline's all-stars invaded the Shore for a game against the local Cambridge Clippers who included within their lineup former Cambridge Dodger Hank Parker and AAA pitcher Charlie Blades. Kaline even had a couple of ex-ESLers on his barnstorming team—Mickey Vernon and Spider Wilhelm. That October 9, 1955, saw the finest collection of professional baseball players on the same field on the Eastern Shore since the famed Phillips Delicious–Coca-Cola city championship of 1936. In addition to Vernon, Kaline, and Wilhelm, the lineups that night also included Lou Grasmick, Ray Moore, Hal Smith, Gus Triandos, Lou Sleater, Russ Kerns, Howie Moss, Bobby Young, and Ted Sepkowski.

And into the bargain of 1955 were contests in Cambridge with the Clippers against the Indianapolis Clowns and the New York Black Yankees as well as a Delmarva pilgrimage to Baltimore in June for Home Run Baker Day at Memorial Stadium.

In 1956 even worldly-wise Eastern Shore folks were struck with wonder when rumors leaked out that a move had been made to bring the professional Eastern Shore League back to life for a fourth time. In September of that year Roy Mack, son of Hall of Famer Connie Mack and vice-president of the Kansas City Athletics (the farm club for the Philadelphia Athletics) met on several occasions with Fred Lucas of Cambridge and baseball's minor league Chairman of Operations George M. Trautman. Also involved in the attempted revival was former ESL player and manager and native of Cambridge Jake Flowers. While Mack, Lucas, and Trautman attempted to cover ground on some basic administrative arrangement, Flowers labored shoulder to shoulder with New York Yankee Farm Director Lee McPhail to garner individual teams' interest.

Local representatives in Cambridge, Salisbury, and Milford felt assured they had the blessing and financial support of major league teams in the effort to resurrect the Eastern Shore League, but other interested towns were not as fortunate or successful in their attempts to sell the idea to prospective clubs. Obviously, three teams would not constitute a reasonable league. So, for all practical purposes, that 1956 effort was the last legitimate attempt to have a professional organized minor league on the Eastern Shore under the auspices of major league baseball.

The spirit of the Eastern Shore League, however, continued to flourish in areas other than the playing field, kept alive by the success of native-born and adopted former ESL players. Sheriff Robinson was promoted to manager of the AA Oklahoma City team by 1957. Reds Griffith of Mardela posted a 14–10 mound record with Elmira of the New York-Penn League during his rookie season in pro ball. Bullet Bob Turley and Danny Murtaugh visited Cambridge as guests of the local Prep League. Twinkletoes Selkirk visited the town where his baseball career had begun. Jake Flowers had a youth league named after him in Salisbury. Home Run Baker had a league named after him in his native Talbot County. What! No Jimmie Foxx League?

Endless articles on the three lives of the Eastern Shore League continued to appear in local newspapers. Usually all manner of stories were told, like the one about Cambridge Canner outfielder Cutter Drury (1922–23) teaching Eddie Rommel (major league pitcher and umpire) how to throw a knuckleball.

More barnstorming teams—teams such as the famed House of David club as well as the Ft. Meade Generals with Dave Sisler on the mound—came to the Shore to take on the local town teams on a number of occasions.

Delmarva natives still made it to the major leagues without the benefit of taking the first step in a friendly local minor league system. Chuck Churn of Bridgetown, Va., debuted with the Pirates in 1957. Forrest "Spook" Jacobs returned to his native Delaware after a four-year assignment with the Athletics.

Chris Short of Milford, Del., enjoyed a sparkling major league career that started in 1959. Bruce Howard of Salisbury, Md., joined the Chicago White Sox in 1963. Costen Shockley of Georgetown, Del., signed with the Phillies in 1964. John Morris of Lewes, Del., labored for six years in the minors before making it with the Phillies in 1966. In 1977 Renie Martin of Dover, Del., was selected by the Kansas City Royals in the amateur free agent draft.

According to the old hands of Delmarva baseball the next Home Run Baker, Mickey Cochrane, Jimmie Foxx, and Judy Johnson counterpart was the number one draft choice of the Chicago White Sox in 1977, one Harold Baines of St. Michaels, Md.; and if his first eight years in the major leagues is any indication of his apparent future he will undoubtedly continue his course to Cooperstown.

Of course many other obscure baseball players from the little towns of Delmarva, like the thousands from hamlets across the country, attempted to attain the ultimate dream, but rarely survived beyond Class A competition. Names like Wayne Todd, Dickie Moore, Brice Kinnamon, George Nichols, Ron Daniels, Bob "Tuffy" Bradway, and Jackie Mills will never appear in *The Sporting News Official Baseball Register*, but they put their dreams on trial and learned firsthand how the ball bounces.

The official Class D Eastern Shore League has been gone for 39 years in reality, but it remains forever in the hearts and souls of Sho' persons. The typical Delmarva yarns and memories associated with the once "fastest Class D baseball league in the country" will live through eternity.

As I indicated in the preface, this book is intended to be a testimonial to the game of baseball and a historical account of the Eastern Shore League. It is an appreciative declaration of devotion to such Delmarva locales as Parksley, Va., and its beloved Spuds; Cambridge, Md., and its infamous Canners; and the one truly forgotten Eastern Shore League team of Northampton, Va., which operated but one season, and is probably even forgotten as the home of the oldest recorded organized protest against taxation without representation in America (irate Northampton citizens objected to a tax on tobacco without representation in the Assembly at Jamestown in 1652).

Geologically speaking the Delmarva Peninsula is a mere 55 million years young and this Sho'man figures that 15 years of the Eastern Shore League under the auspices of major league baseball is but a beginning as opposed to the end in 1949. After all, Hagerstown, Md., has its minor Carolina League Suns—so who knows what is coming in the way of baseball for the Shore in the future.

1946 Eastern Shore League

Team	Won	Lost	Pct.
Centreville, Md.	88	37	.704
Milford, Del.	77	49	.611
Dover, Del.	68	57	.544
Salisbury, Md.	61	64	.488
Easton, Md.	59	66	.472
Seaford, Del.	58	68	.460
Cambridge, Md.	53	73	.421
Federalsburg, Md.	37	87	.298

Individual Pitching	IP	BB	SO	W	L	Pct.	G	CG	ERA
Heuser, Centreville	49	17	34	6	0	1.000	7	5	1.10
Markell, Seaford	85	36	88	5	5	.500	13	8	1.59
Deal, Milford	88	18	51	7	3	.700	12	8	2.15
DeForge, Cambridge	127	14	66	8	6	.571	23	10	2.48
Parker, Milford	97	62	82	7	4	.636	13	8	2.51
Bournot, Cambridge	91	69	98	8	4	.667	12	7	2.67
Coulling, Centreville	203	28	81	17	8	.680	31	19	2.88
Cave, Centreville	187	90	173	14	8	.636	24	17	2.89
Kitterman, Milford	73	39	41	5	2	.714	14	3	2.90
Beringer, Cambridge	192	54	114	8	13	.381	29	16	3.09

Poholsky, Milford	141	34	75	9	4	.692	23	12	3.64
Krausse, Federalsburg	216	31	72	11	12	.478	29	21	4.26

Individual Batting	G	AB	R	H	Avg.	HR	RBI	TB
Higdon, Dover	38	139	43	52	.374	6	26	82
Wollgast, Salisbury	41	87	10	32	.368	0	16	37
Havelka, Federalsburg	69	238	49	86	.361	3	29	116
Langston, Salisbury	84	346	44	122	.353	5	65	172
Millies, Milford	40	116	26	41	.353	2	15	57
Pacitto, Centreville	119	479	102	164	.342	0	79	221
Malfara, Centreville	119	474	103	162	.342	10	99	232
DeLucca, Seaford	94	351	88	119	.339	3	23	159
Kiel, Dover	95	339	65	115	.339	25	90	214
Marshall, Dover	122	486	108	161	.331	29	110	280
Contini, Salisbury	127	477	98	143	.300	4	59	183
Becker, Seaford	37	100	17	28	.280	2	14	38
Bilko, Salisbury	122	441	73	121	.274	12	90	193

1947 Eastern Shore League

Team	Won	Lost	Pct.	Regular Attendance	Play-off Attendance
Cambridge, Md.	91	34	.728	62,118	18,746
Seaford, Del.	74	49	.602	54,637	12,630
Dover, Del.	68	57	.544	33,676	5,748
Federalsburg, Md.	62	63	.496	29,781	2,684
Milford, Del.	62	64	.492	29,581	
Rehoboth Beach, Del.	50	75	.400	30,521	
Easton, Md.	48	78	.381	42,618	
Salisbury, Md.	45	90	.360	51,739	
Total				334,671	

Individual Pitching	IP	BB	SO	W	L	Pct.	G	CG	ERA
Van Cuyk, Cambridge	233	85	279	25	2	.926	31	24	1.94
Beringer, Cambridge	237	65	179	22	6	.786	31	22	2.55
Muir, Rehoboth Beach	162	46	134	13	5	.722	22	16	2.84
Andre, Seaford	179	103	108	15	6	.714	34	14	3.27
Markell, Seaford	249	110	274	19	9	.679	37	24	3.51
George, Dover	182	102	167	15	5	.750	25	14	3.56
Moford, Salisbury	105	48	63	5	9	.357	18	5	3.86
Quill, Cambridge	206	129	124	18	3	.857	28	17	3.98

Individual Batting	G	AB	R	H	Avg.	HR	RBI	TB
Rambert, Federalsburg	97	367	72	138	.376	19	100	138
Nichols, Cambridge	123	448	97	159	.355	3	130	215
Detweiler, Federalsburg	118	423	110	149	.352	29	133	269
Thompson, Cambridge	114	464	101	162	.349	3	129	219
Ripken, Cambridge	97	381	103	132	.347	5	75	184
McKinnon, Seaford	114	422	99	145	.344	7	90	194
Ford, Seaford	120	442	97	151	.342	3	98	197
Westfall, Seaford	121	449	96	153	.341	14	121	231
Contini, Salisbury	84	320	63	109	.341	1	45	137
Stramm, Cambridge	123	477	129	162	.340	4	84	210

1948 Eastern Shore League

Team	Won	Lost	Pct.	Regular Attendance	Play-off Attendance
Salisbury, Md.	89	32	.736	59,164	7,015
Milford, Del.	81	43	.653	21,967	8,296
Easton, Md.	71	50	.587	37,780	5,619
Cambridge, Md.	65	61	.516	31,737	9,709
Rehoboth Beach, Del.	60	65	.480	21,845	
Seaford, Del.	56	70	.444	31,850	
Federalsburg, Md.	49	76	.392	22,901	
Dover, Del.	26	100	.206	10,079	
Total				237,323	30,639

Individual Pitching	IP	BB	SO	W	L	Pct.	G	CG	ERA
Black, Salisbury	194	79	179	16	5	.762	23	18	2.23
Wollgast, Salisbury	207	76	167	17	6	.739	31	22	2.26
Moford, Salisbury	207	74	129	20	4	.833	26	19	2.39
Kern, Cambridge	104	47	87	9	3	.750	17	10	2.60
Perry, Milford	110	77	149	9	3	.750	14	12	2.62
Hall, Milford	184	66	136	16	4	.800	24	19	2.93
Margeit, Cambridge	195	79	85	9	12	.429	30	13	3.05
Loveness, Rehoboth	133	35	82	9	5	.643	21	9	3.11

Adams, Federalsburg	189	77	169	11	10	.524	27	16	3.19
Andre, Seaford	263	148	228	21	12	.636	34	29	3.35

Individual Batting	G	AB	R	H	Avg.	HR	RBI	TB
Maxa, Easton	91	353	103	135	.382	8	87	187
Jablonski, Milford	123	486	108	172	.354	26	131	278
Zauchin, Milford	120	481	126	170	.353	33	138	324
Detweiler, Federalsburg	110	369	86	126	.341	21	95	219
Price, Milford	84	343	71	117	.341	19	96	219
Ford, Seaford	111	370	78	126	.340	10	91	190
Davidson, Easton	93	352	95	118	.335	21	111	217
Hofferth, Cambridge	62	206	38	69	.335	1	47	95
Quartararo, Easton	104	404	110	132	.327	3	68	172
Rivera, Salisbury	111	455	72	147	.323	3	83	189
Westfall, Seaford	49	173	36	56	.323	5	44	88
Malzone, Milford	120	424	107	129	.304	10	77	199

1949 Eastern Shore League

Team	Won	Lost	Pct.	GB	Regular Attendance	Play-off Attendance
Easton, Md.	68	52	.567	–	38,651	
Federalsburg, Md.	63	56	.529	4½	30,139	
Salisbury, Md.	60	59	.504	7½	39,063	
Rehoboth Beach, Del.	56	63	.471	11½	22,358	
Seaford, Del.	56	64	.467	12	35,519	
Cambridge, Md.	55	64	.462	12½	29,434	
Total					195,164	18,386

Individual Pitching	IP	BB	SO	W	L	Pct.	G	CG	ERA
Markel, Seaford	108	54	118	10	1	.909	14	11	2.17
Zeisz, Cambridge	140	85	118	10	7	.588	21	12	2.38
Baker, Federalsburg	181	78	100	14	5	.737	41	6	2.59
Rimmey, Salisbury	157	109	121	12	5	.706	27	9	4.19
Burnette, Easton	169	88	102	13	6	.684	26	15	2.77
DeAngelo, Easton	136	74	147	10	5	.667	20	11	3.64
Benedict, Salisbury	89	71	51	6	3	.667	17	4	4.14
McCrea, Federalsburg	151	84	101	11	6	.647	25	11	4.53
Andre, Rehoboth Beach	249	126	240	17	11	.607	29	24	2.74
Miller, Salisbury	151	90	97	8	13	.381	29	8	4.29

Individual Batting	G	AB	R	H	Avg.	HR	RBI	TB
Bragg, Easton	94	348	70	126	.362	5	42	167
Westfall, Federalsburg	120	445	126	158	.355	19	113	260
Dickey, Salisbury	82	271	93	94	.347	13	45	162
Detweiler, Federalsburg	103	375	89	127	.339	13	107	206
Smith, Federalsburg	81	327	83	111	.339	6	40	153
Corbett, Salisbury	94	315	53	102	.324	9	68	153
Catallo, Seaford	84	312	62	99	.317	5	50	145
Etichison, Federalsburg	80	304	71	95	.313	6	59	113
Gaulin, Seaford	120	464	90	144	.310	3	53	182
Anderson, Easton	107	410	52	127	.310	0	58	153
Hamric, Cambridge	62	138	20	37	.268	1	18	48
Pignatano, Cambridge	87	268	51	62	.232	0	24	77
Zimmer, Cambridge	71	304	56	69	.228	4	30	101

Part II

Biographies

The following is an alphabetical listing and profiles of players, managers, coaches, umpires, scouts, and administrators with Eastern Shore League ties who were also associated with major league baseball during their careers.

Those preceded by an asterisk are Delmarva natives who have been associated with major league baseball, but not with the ESL.

ANDRE, John Edward "Long John"
Born: 1-3-23, Brockton, Mass.
Died: 11-25-76, Centerville, Mass.
BL   TR   6'4"   200 lbs.
ESL: Seaford, Del. (1947–48), Rehoboth Beach, Del. (1949)
Major Leagues: Chicago Cubs (1955)
Position: P
Career Record: 0–1

Andre held the ESL record (tied with Les Hinckle of Federalsburg) for complete games in a season (29), set in 1948. In addition, that same season he set records for most hits allowed (272) and for walks (148). He was also an excellent pinch hitter while in the ESL.

   Andre lost his only big league decision with the '55 Cubs. He once faced Roy Campanella (the only batter he faced in the game) and had him hit into a triple play. He was a boyhood friend of former world heavyweight boxing champ Rocky Marciano.

ANTOLICK, Joseph
Born: 4-11-16, Hokendauqua, Penna.
Address: 723 2nd St., Catasauqua, Penna. 18032
BR   TR   6'   185 lbs.
ESL: Easton, Md. (1947)
Major Leagues: Philadelphia Phillies (1944)
Position: Player/Manager
Career Average: .333

Joe appeared in four major league games for the 1944 Phillies and was 2 for 6 at the plate. After completing his major league playing career, he came to the Eastern Shore League as manager of the Easton Club in 1947.

ARMSTRONG, Herbert E. "Herb"
Died: 7-28-84, Baltimore, Md.
ESL: Cambridge, Md. (1922–24), Crisfield, Md. (1925)
Major Leagues: Baltimore Orioles (1953–72)
Position: 1B/Manager/Business Manager/President of the Orioles Foundation

The most playing time Herb got in the Eastern Shore League was during its initial season in 1922 when he was player/manager for the Cambridge Canners. He appeared in 67 games that year, hitting .249 with 91 total bases.

   Herb joined the International League Orioles as vice-president in 1943, and was named business manager of the Orioles when they came to Baltimore with the American League in late 1953.

   President of the Maryland Scholastic Association for 14 years, he was associated with the group for 55 years. Armstrong graduated from Tufts College in 1916.

*BAINES, Harold Douglass
Born: 3-15-59, Easton, Md.
Address: 107 Trusty St., St. Michaels, Md.
       21663
BL   TL   6'2"   195 lbs.
Major Leagues:
  Chicago White Sox (1980–current)
Position: OF
Career Average: .288

Baines was the first player selected in the free agent draft on June 7, 1977.

He tied the major league record for most plate appearances in a game (12) and tied the American League record for longest errorless game and most innings by an outfielder (25) in a game that started on May 8, went 25 innings, and was completed on May 9, 1984. Also in 1984, Baines led the American League in slugging percentage with .541. In 1985, this young outfielder established the American League record for most game-winning runs batted in for a season (22).

Baines hit three home runs in games on July 17, 1982, and September 17, 1984; he played in the 1983 American League championship series; and was named to the American League all-star team in 1985, '86, and '87. An injury in 1987 continued to nag Baines in 1988 and he saw most action as a designated hitter.

FRANK "HOMERUN" BAKER

BAKER, John Franklin "Home Run"
Born: 3-13-86, Trappe, Md.
Died: 6-28-63, Trappe, Md.
BL   TR   5'11"   173 lbs.
ESL: Easton, Md. (1924)
Major Leagues:
    Philadelphia A's (1908–14)
    New York Yankees (1916–22)
Position: 3B/Manager
Career Average: .307

Baker earned his nickname "Home Run" when he hit two game-winning home runs during the 1911 World Series.

Home Run played in the majors for 13 years and appeared in six World Series, hitting .363 in 25 games. He never played any other position than 3B (1,570 games). Baker was the third baseman of Connie Mack's famous $100,000 infield, along with Stuffy McInnis (1B), Eddie Collins (2B), and Jack Barry (SS); they were together for four years, 1911–14. Home Run was the home run leader for his decade (1910–19), hitting 76 round-trippers.

Brother Gilbert, who was director of athletics at Mount St. Joseph's in Baltimore, is often credited with discovering Baker, and Babe Ruth as well. The two players were on opposing teams when they met on March 25, 1914, in an exhibition game at Wilmington, N.C. Baker was playing with the Orioles (they trained in Fayetteville), and the Babe was pitching for the world champion A's (remember, he was initially a hurler before becoming a slugger). Ruth hurled a 6–2 victory, but not before Frank Baker tagged the Bambino for four hits (a double and three singles). Baker ranks second to Ruth for hitting the most home runs off Walter Johnson, tagging "the Big Train" for five homers (Ruth hit 10 off Johnson).

Frank Baker came to Easton in 1924 as player/manager and hit .293 with five home runs in but 43 games. Also while in the ESL he discovered and managed future Hall of Famer Jimmy Foxx. Today there is a league named after him in his native Talbot County.

Biographies

BECKER, Joseph Edward "Joe"
Born: 6-25-09, St. Louis, Mo.
Address: 2800 21st Place, Vero Beach, Fla. 32960
BR   TR   6'1"   180 lbs.
ESL: Seaford, Del. (1946)
Major Leagues: Cleveland Indians (1936–37)
Position: Player/Manager
Career Average: .241

Becker was an active professional baseball player from 1930 until 1949. He was in 40 games during his two years as an active player in the major leagues, hitting .333 (11 for 33) in 1937 with the Cleveland Indians.

Joe came to the Eastern Shore League in 1946 as player/co-manager with Walter Youse of the Seaford Eagles. He appeared in 37 ESL games and hit .280 that season.

Starting his coaching career in the major leagues with the Brooklyn Dodgers (1955–57), he continued in the majors with the following teams: Los Angeles Dodgers (1958–64), St. Louis Cardinals (1965–66), and Chicago Cubs (1967–70).

BERINGER, Carroll James "C.B."
Born: 8-14-28, Bellwood, Nebr.
Address: 4917 Granite Shoals, Fort Worth, Tex. 76103
BR   TR   6'   195 lbs.
ESL: Cambridge, Md. (1946–47)
Major Leagues: Los Angeles Dodgers (1961–72), Philadelphia Phillies (1973)
Position: Batting Practice Pitcher/Coach

C.B. had a super year with the 1947 Cambridge Dodger championship club, chalking up a 22–6 record with a 2.55 ERA. He worked in 31 games with 22 complete games and 237 innings pitched. In 1959, Beringer was named pitcher of the year at Victoria of the Texas League, when he led the league with 19 complete games.

In terms of association with one major league club, Beringer ranks up there with Walt Alston and Tom Lasorda in tenure with the Dodgers, but it all started in the Eastern Shore League in 1946 at Cambridge.

*BETTS, Walter Martin "Huck"
Born: 2-18-97, Millsboro, Del.
Died: 6-13-87, Millsboro, Del.
BL   TR   5'11"   170 lbs.
Major Leagues: Philadelphia Phillies (1920–25), Boston Braves (1932–35)
Position: P
Career Record: 61–68

Betts pitched in the major leagues for 10 years, with his best season coming in 1934, when he recorded a 17–10 record for the Boston Braves. (He was 13–11 for the '32 Braves with a 2.80 ERA.)

The nickname "Huck" was given to him by shortstop Dave Bancroft in his rookie year (1920) with the Phillies. The Phils were on a train south to spring training when Bancroft spotted this shy-looking youngster sitting by himself and remarked, "Why, look who's with us—a Huckleberry Finn!"

Betts retired from baseball after a 2–9 season for the Braves in 1935, rather than take a demotion to the minors. He returned to his hometown and purchased a movie house which he called the Ball Theatre (it had a baseball replica on top).

BEVAN, Harold Joseph "Hal"
Born: 11-15-30, New Orleans, La.
Died: 10-5-68, New Orleans, La.
BR   TR   6'2"   198 lbs.
ESL: Rehoboth, Del. (1948)
Major Leagues:
  Boston Red Sox (1952)
  Philadelphia Athletics (1952)
  Kansas City Athletics (1955)
  Cincinnati Reds (1961)
Position: C
Career Average: .292

Hal truly loved the game of baseball. He spent 14 years in the minor leagues and had four great years at Seattle of the Pacific Coast League (1957–60), hitting 23 home runs there in '57 before joining the Reds in '61. Despite playing with four different major league teams spanning a nine-year period, he appeared in only 15 big league games.

STEVE BILKO
First Base — Los Angeles Angels

BILKO, Stephen Thomas "Steve"
Born: 11-13-28, Wilkes-Barre, Penna.
Died: 3-7-78, Wilkes-Barre, Penna.
BR   TR   6'1"   230 lbs.
ESL: Salisbury, Md. (1946)
Major Leagues:
  St. Louis Cards (1949–53)
  Chicago Cubs (1954)
  Cincinnati Reds/Los Angeles Dodgers
    (1958)
  Detroit Tigers (1960)
  Los Angeles Angels (1961–62)
Position: 1B
Career Average: .249

Bilko played in 600 major league games. His best power year was 1953, when he hit 21 home runs and had 84 RBIs for the Cardinals. Described as one of the greatest minor league players in baseball history, he won the minor league triple crown in 1956.

For the '46 Salisbury team, Steve hit .274 with 12 home runs, 90 RBIs, and 193 total bases. He appeared in 122 games for Salisbury's ESL team.

BOYER, James Murray "Jim"
Born: 4-21-09, Templeville, Md.
Died: 7-25-59, Finksburg, Md.
ESL: 1937
Major Leagues: American League (1944–49)
Position: Umpire

Jim was an Eastern Shore product, born in Caroline County.

BRADY, Robert Jay "Bob"
Born: 11-8-22, Lewistown, Penna.
Address: 42 Overland St., Manchester, Conn. 06040
BL   TR   6'1"   175 lbs.
ESL: Salisbury, Md. (1937)
Major Leagues: Boston Braves (1946–47)
Position: C
Career Average: .167

The forgotten man of the famed 1937 Salisbury Indians who captured the ESL pennant after forfeiting their first 21 victories, Bob Brady was the cause of the forfeiture, playing first base in violation of the "class player" rule.

Brady played in four games in the major leagues, coming to the plate six times and collecting one hit over a two-year period. He caught one game for the Braves.

BRENNAN, John "Dutch"
Born: Baltimore, Md.
ESL: Cambridge, Md. (1922)
Major Leagues: Brooklyn Dodgers (1945–46), Philadelphia Athletics (1947–?)
Position: Scout

Dutch actually began his baseball career on the Eastern Shore prior to the first official ESL season of 1922. He played with the independent teams of Queenstown, Centreville, and Salisbury in 1919–21 before a short stint with the Cambridge Canners of the ESL in 1922. Starting his umpiring career in the ESL in 1923, Brennan later moved on to other leagues: Virginia, Three I, South Atlantic, and Mid-Atlantic. He also helped revive the Eastern Shore League in 1937.

Brennan joined the scouting staff of the Brooklyn Dodgers for 1945 and '46. He then moved over to the Philadelphia Athletics as a scout.

BROWN, Clinton Harold "Clint"
Born: 7-8-03, Blackash, Penna.
Died: 12-31-55, Rocky River, Ohio
BL   TR   6'1"   190 lbs.
ESL: Cambridge, Md. (1926), Parksley, Va. (1927)
Major Leagues: Cleveland Indians (1928–35), Chicago White Sox (1936–40), Cleveland
                    Indians (1941–42)
Position: P
Career Record: 89–92

Clint pitched in the major leagues for 15 years. His best season was for the 1932 Cleveland Indians when he compiled a 15–12 record. He became strictly a relief pitcher in 1937 and never started another major league game, but had 18 saves his first year as a fireman. In 1939 while with the Chicago White Sox he compiled an 11–10 record with 18 saves.

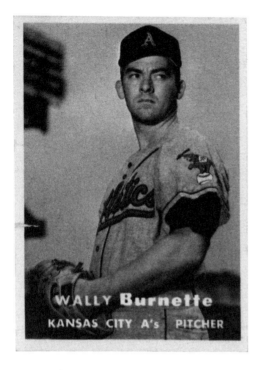

BURNETTE, Wallace Harper "Wally"
Born: 6-20-29, Blairs, Va.
Address: RR 1, Box 168, Blairs, Va. 24527
BR   TR   6'1/2"   178 lbs.
ESL: Easton, Md. (1949)
Major Leagues:
  Kansas City Athletics (1956–58)
Position: P
Career Record: 14–21

Burnette started his baseball career (following two years of military service) with the Easton Yankees in 1949, helping Easton to the ESL pennant with a 13–6 record. Altogether that year he had 15 complete games and pitched 169 innings with 102 strikeouts and a 2.77 ERA.

Wally won 21 games with Binghamton in '53, 12 with K.C. in '54, and 15 with Denver in '55.

He started in 14 games his rookie season in 1956 with Kansas City and had a respectable 2.89 ERA, although he compiled a 6–8 record. Today he owns Burnette's Grocery and Sandwich Shop in Blairs, Va.

CATHER, Theodore P.
Born: 5-20-89, Chester, Penna.
Died: 4-9-45, Charlestown, Md.
BR   TR   5'10½"   178 lbs.
ESL: Easton, Md. (1926–27)
Major Leagues: St. Louis Cardinals (1912–14), Boston Braves (1914–15)
Position: OF/Manager
Career Average: .252

Ted enjoyed his best major league season in 1914 even though he split the season between the Cardinals and the Braves, hitting .287 in 89 games as an outfielder with 40 RBIs. He also appeared in one World Series game, going 0 for 5.

Joining Easton as player/manager in 1926, he led the ESL in doubles that year with 31. He hit .322 in 79 games, including 156 total bases, in 1927.

*CHURN, Clarence Nottingham "Chuck"
Born: 2-1-30, Bridgetown, Va.
Address: Box 39, Greenbush, Va. 23357
BR   TR   6'3"   205 lbs.
Major Leagues: Pittsburgh Pirates (1957), Cleveland Indians (1958), Los Angeles
                  Dodgers (1959)
Position: P
Career Record: 3–2

Churn broke in with the Pittsburgh Pirates in 1957, appearing in five games without a decision. He went to the Cleveland Indians in '58 and saw action in six games without a decision. Chuck got into one World Series game for the championship Los Angeles Dodgers of 1959 and ended his major league career that year, posting a 3–2 mark with a 4.99 ERA. His entire record was in relief and he also had one save. He returned to the Eastern Shore of Virginia and is now a farmer.

A neat trivia fact is that Chuck was the winning pitcher in the game that broke the long winning streak of Pirates relief ace Roy Face, who had won 17 consecutive games in 1959.

CLARK, Alfred Aloysius "Allie"
Born: 6-16-23, South Amboy, N.J.
Address: 250 N. Stevens Ave., South
　　　　　Amboy, N.J. 08879
BR　　TR　　6′　　185 lbs.
ESL: Easton, Md.
Major Leagues:
　New York Yankees (1947)
　Cleveland Indians (1948–51)
　Philadelphia Athletics (1951–53)
　Chicago White Sox (1953)
Position: OF
Career Average: .262

Allie was with two World Series-winning teams in his first two years in the major leagues. He hit .373 with the Yankees while winning the '47 series (1 for 2 in the series) and hit .310 the following year with the world champion Indians. Clark also hit .333 as a pinch hitter for the 1952 Philadelphia Athletics.

In the 1941 Eastern Shore League, he helped Easton to a third-place finish.

CLARKE, Jay Justin "Nig"
Born: 12-15-82, Amherstburg, Ont., Canada
Died: 6-15-49, Detroit, Mich.
BL　　TR
ESL: Salisbury, Md. (1925)
Major Leagues: Cleveland Indians (1905–10), St. Louis Browns (1911), Philadelphia
　　　　　　　Phillies (1919), Pittsburgh Pirates (1920)
Position: C
Career Average: .254

Clarke's most productive major league year was with the 1907 Cleveland Indians, when he played in 120 games, collected 105 hits for a .269 average, and had 19 doubles and 33 RBIs. In 1906 he hit .358 in 57 games for the Indians.

Nig came to the Eastern Shore League in 1925 with Salisbury and appeared in 81 games, batting .276 with 33 runs scored and 96 total bases.

Playing for Corsicana in a Texas League game on June 15, 1902, he was involved in one of the wildest baseball games in history and recorded an amazing batting feat: He hit 8 home runs and had 16 RBIs in a 51–3 victory over Texarkana.

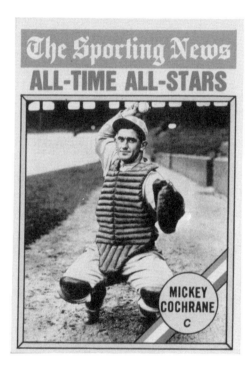

COCHRANE, Gordon Stanley "Mickey"
Born: 4-6-03, Bridgewater, Mass.
Died: 6-28-62, Lake Forest, Ill.
BL   TR   5'10½"   180 lbs.
ESL: Dover, Del. (1923)
Major Leagues:
   Philadelphia Athletics (1925–33)
   Detroit Tigers (1934–37)
Position: C
Career Average: .320

Mickey Cochrane played under the name Frank King in the ESL for Dover. In 65 games he logged 115 total bases with five home runs to help Dover to the pennant.

On April 14, 1925, 22,000 spectators at Shibe Park had the singular treat of watching two future Hall of Famers debut together in their first major league game, for the same team. Mickey Cochrane shared the catching duties with Cy Perkins for the A's and contributed a single in his two turns at bat. Lefty Grove (spelled Groves in those days) started rather inauspiciously, walking four batters and hitting one.

Considered by many to have been the best all-around catcher in baseball history, Mickey caught in over 100 games per year for 11 consecutive years (a total of 1,451 games), played one game in the outfield, took part in five World Series, and was the American League's MVP in 1928.

In the long history of the major leagues, only eight managers have been able to win pennants in their first two, three, or four full years. Player/manager Mickey Cochrane took the Detroit Tigers to pennants his first two years, 1934 and 1935. He also managed the Tigers to the world championship in 1935.

On May 25, 1937, in a game against the Yankees, catcher/manager Cochrane was seriously beaned by pitcher Bump Hadley. A fractured skull ended his playing career. However, as manager, Cochrane then had to decide who—among Ray Hayworth, Birdie Tebbetts, and Rudy York—would catch. On August 4, following a six-game losing streak, York was inserted on a full-time basis and responded with an August of record proportions. In 30 games he hit 18 home runs, scored 27 runs, and hit .360 with 4 doubles, 2 triples, and a .895 slugging percentage.

COLLINS, Joseph Edward "Joe"
Born: 12-3-22, Scranton, Penna.
Address: 731 Suburban Rd., Union, N.J.
    07083
BL   TL   6′   185 lbs.
ESL: Easton, Md. (1939)
Major Leagues:
    New York Yankees (1948–57)
Position: 1B
Career Average: .256

Born Joseph Edward Kollonige, Joe played in 36 games in a total of 7 World Series for Casey Stengel's Yankees. He hit two home runs against the Dodgers in the series opener in '55. Collins spent all 10 years he was in the majors with the Yankees. In 1952, he hit .280 and rapped 18 home runs. He collected over 100 hits in both 1952 and 1953.

COLLINS, Thomas Patrick "Jocko"
ESL: Crisfield, Md. (1927)
Major Leagues: Philadelphia Phillies (1940–69), New York Mets (1970–80)
Position: IF/Scout

Jocko joined the Crisfield Crabbers of the ESL as an infielder in 1927 fresh out of St. Joseph's College.

   After his playing days were ended he went to work at a post office and one day recommended a local prospect to Phillie scout Gerrie Nugent, who in turn hired Collins as a scout for the Phillies. He worked the mid-Atlantic area for many years.

COMELLAS, Jorge "Pancho"
Born: 12-18-17, Havana, Cuba
Address: 13015 SW 50th St., Miami, Fla. 33165
BR   TR   6′   185 lbs.
ESL: Salisbury, Md. (1937–40)
Major Leagues: Chicago Cubs (1945)
Position: P
Career Record: 0–2

Pancho's best year in professional baseball was with the ESL's Salisbury club in 1938 when he fashioned a 22–1 record. He came back again two years later to etch a 21–10 mark—to lead the league both years. He also led the Eastern Shore League in innings pitched in 1940—he worked 258 total innings.

   In the majors, Comellas pitched in seven games for the 1945 Cubs, including one start. He walked six and struck out six in his brief major league career.

CORBETT, Eugene Louis "Gene"
Born: 10-25-13, Winona, Minn.
Address: Box 904, Salisbury, Md. 21801
BL   TR   6′1½″   190 lbs.
ESL: Salisbury, Md. (1948–49)
Major Leagues: Philadelphia Phillies (1936–38)
Position: 1B/ Manager
Career Average: .120

Gene came to the Eastern Shore League as player/manager of the Salisbury Cardinals in 1948 and promptly led the Redbirds to the ESL pennant with the best winning percentage in professional baseball that year, at .736 (89–32), setting an ESL record.

   At age 34 Gene was also still able to show the youngsters some hitting pointers, logging a .270 batting average over a 114-game stretch with 83 RBIs; he was a defensive gem with but five errors at first base in 1,056 chances.

   Gene played in 37 games over a three-year period, with 1938 being his most productive major league season—he appeared in 24 games and went 6 for 75 (.080). He was also, at one time, International League batting champion.

DASCOLI, Frank
Born: Canterbury, Conn.
Address: Box 75, Danielson, Conn.
06239
ESL: 1946
Major Leagues:
National League (1948–61)
Position: Umpire

After serving two years in the U.S. Coast Guard during World War II, Frank Dascoli started his career in the Eastern Shore League in 1946 and then went on to the Canadian American League in 1947. He joined the National League umpiring staff on the Fourth of July, 1948, moving up from the International League. Frank worked the 1951 all-star game and the 1953 World Series.

DETWEILER, Robert Sterling "Ducky"
Born: 2-15-19, Trumbauersville, Penna.
Address: 312 Holt St., Federalsburg, Md. 21632
BR   TR   5′11″   178 lbs.
ESL: Federalsburg, Md. (1939, 1947–49)
Major Leagues: Boston Braves (1942, '46)
Position: 3B
Career Average: .311

Detweiler had a 40-game hitting streak in 1938 while playing with the Evansville Bees, collecting 74 hits and batting over .400 during the string.

He hit the first pitch ever thrown to him as a major leaguer for a single and proceeded that day to go 3 for 7 in a doubleheader for his big league debut. During his rookie year with the Braves ('42), Ducky went 14 for 44 (.318) but, like many young ballplayers of the time, his bright career was interrupted from 1943 to 1945 for the military.

The year of his return to the ESL, he was named the Eastern Shore League's Most Valuable Player (1947) with some impressive statistics: 29 home runs, 133 RBIs, and 269 total bases. Ducky also had an 18-game hitting streak in the ESL in 1948, going 26 for 65.

DONAHUE, John Frederick "Jiggs"
Born: 4-19-94, Roxbury, Mass.
Died: 10-3-49, Boston, Mass.
BL   TR   5'8"   170 lbs.
ESL: Dover, Del. (1924)
Major Leagues: Boston Red Sox (1923)
Position: C/Manager
Career Average: .278

After playing in 10 games for the Red Sox in 1923 and going 10 for 36 with four doubles, Jiggs came to the Eastern Shore League as manager of the Dover club. There, he caught 60 games and hit .244 on the season.

DUNN, Jack, III
Born: 10-22-21, Baltimore, Md.
Died: 6-11-87, Baltimore, Md.
ESL: Centreville, Md. (1946)
Position: Player/General Manager
Major Leagues: Baltimore Orioles (1954–1987)
Position: Vice-President Stadium Operations/Board of Directors

Jack appeared as a player in less than 10 games for the Centreville Orioles in 1946 but he was satisfied with his general manager position, as the O's won the '46 ESL pennant.

After being elevated to the Baltimore Orioles he served in most of the front office positions, including traveling secretary, assistant to the general manager, public relations director, play-by-play broadcaster, and administrative assistant to Lee McPhail prior to earning the position of vice-president.

He was the grandson of the late Jack Dunn who owned and managed the International League Orioles to seven straight pennants from 1919 to 1925.

Jack was a fighter pilot during World War II. In more recent years, he frequently visited the Shore, and in 1969 proudly watched his son Jack IV help Towson's American Legion baseball team win the Maryland state title in Cambridge.

EHLERS, Arthur
Born: 1897, Baltimore, Md.
Died: 2-7-77, Baltimore, Md.
ESL: Pocomoke City, Md. (1937–38)
Major Leagues: Philadelphia Athletics (1948), Baltimore Orioles (1971)
Position: Owner/Minor League Director/Scout

Art was one of the Baltimore scholastic ranks' best pitchers back in 1917 and upon graduation was offered a professional contract by Baltimore Orioles owner Jack Dunn.

The war eventually came and ended his potential baseball career. Art enlisted in the infantry and served with the 111th Machine Gun Battalion of the 29th Division in the

Army. In September 1918 during the Battle of the Argonne a shell almost ripped his leg off and a couple of machine gun blasts hit him in the pitching arm. He was in Walter Reed Hospital for a year and he had to use crutches for two more years afterward.

Ehlers purchased the Pocomoke City ball club independently in 1937 to continue in the sport he loved.

He was later named president of the Interstate League.

In 1942 Ehlers was appointed minor league promotional director and in 1948 became minor league director for the Philadelphia Athletics.

He later became a scout for the Baltimore Orioles.

ETCHISON, Clarence Hampton "Buck"
Born: 1-27-15, Baltimore, Md.
Died: 1-24-80, East New Market, Md.
BL   TL   6'1"   190 lbs.
ESL: Federalsburg, Md. (1949)
Major Leagues: Boston Braves (1943–44)
Position: 1B
Career Average: .220

Buck's major league career with the Boston Braves included a 1944 season in which he played in 109 games, hitting .214 with 16 doubles, eight home runs, and 33 RBIs. Buck came to the Eastern Shore League with Federalsburg in that final year of its operation and appeared in 80 games, hitting .313, with 18 doubles and 113 total bases.

FEINBERG, Eddie "Itzy"
Born: 9-29-18, Philadelphia, Penna.
Died: 4-20-86, Hollywood, Fla.
BB   TR   5'9"   165 lbs.
ESL: Centreville, Md. (1937)
Major Leagues: Philadelphia Phillies (1938–39)
Position: SS
Career Average: .184

With the ESL Centreville club Feinberg hit a hefty .334 in 1937, including 17 doubles and 15 home runs.

Little Itzy appeared in 16 major league games for the Phillies, collecting seven hits in 38 turns at bat.

FISCHER, Charles William "Carl"
Born: 11-5-05, Medina, N.Y.
Died: 12-10-63, Medina, N.Y.
BR   TL   6'   180 lbs.
ESL: Cambridge, Md. (1925)
Major Leagues: Washington Senators (1930–32), St. Louis Browns (1932), Detroit Tigers
              (1933), Chicago White Sox (1933–35), Cleveland Indians (1935),
              Washington Senators (1937)
Position: P
Career Record: 46–50

Carl started and ended his major league career with the Washington Senators. His best year was 1931, when he posted a 13–9 won-lost record.

   Later, for the 1933 Detroit Tigers, he logged a 5–1 mark out of the bull pen and had three saves to his credit.

FITZBERGER, Charles Caspar "Charlie"
Born: 2-13-04, Baltimore, Md.
Died: 1-25-65, Baltimore, Md.
BL   TL   6'1½"   170 lbs.
ESL: Parksley, Va. (1924–25)
Major Leagues: Boston Braves (1928)
Position: PH
Career Average: .286

Charlie appeared in seven games for the 1928 Boston Braves, getting two hits in seven at bats. All seven plate appearances were pinch-hitting roles and he never appeared defensively in the major leagues.

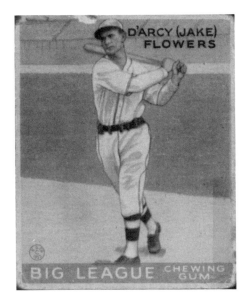

FLOWERS, D'arcy Raymond "Jake"
Born: 3-16-02, Cambridge, Md.
Died: 12-27-62, Clearwater, Fla.
BR   TR   5'11½"   170 lbs.
ESL: Cambridge, Md. (1922), Salisbury,
    Md. (1937–38)
Major Leagues:
  St. Louis Cardinals (1923–26)
  Brooklyn Dodgers (1927–31)
  St. Louis Cardinals (1931–32)
  Brooklyn Dodgers (1933)
  Cincinnati Reds (1934)
Position: 2B/Manager
Career Average: .256

Jake played all four infield positions during his 10 years in the major leagues, but generally is regarded as a second baseman. His best year in the bigs was with the 1930 Dodgers, when he hit a .320 average.

Jake appeared in two World Series. He was named Minor League Manager of the Year by *The Sporting News* in 1937 at Salisbury of the ESL.

Jake was inducted into the Maryland Athletic Hall of Fame in 1977.

JIMMIE FOXX

FOXX, James Emory "Double X"
Born: 10-22-07, Sudlersville, Md.
Died: 7-21-67, Miami, Fla.
BR   TR   6′   195 lbs.
ESL: Easton, Md. (1924)
Major Leagues:
  Philadelphia Athletics (1925–35)
  Boston Red Sox (1936–42)
  Chicago Cubs (1942–44)
  Philadelphia Phillies (1945)
Position: 1B
Career Average: .325

Jimmy Foxx was a great power hitter who hit 30 or more home runs in each of 12 seasons. His name is second on the all-time career leader list for grand-slam home runs (17—Lou Gehrig hit 23); fourth on the all-time list of batters hitting the most home runs in extra inning games (14—Mays had 22, Ruth 16, and Frank Robinson 15); and first on the list for most home runs in the eleventh inning (6). Only two of Foxx's 534 career home runs were inside-the-park homers.

A born and bred Delmarva athlete, Jimmy was discovered in 1924 by Easton Manager Frank Baker and in his only year with the ESL hit .296 under Manager Baker. The next year, 1925, he was the youngest player in the major leagues at age 17. He played in the majors for 20 years, starting out right by belting 10 home runs in his first professional season.

In 1932 Jimmy hit 58 home runs, scored 151 runs, and had 169 RBIs. This earned him the American League MVP award for 1932, an honor he was to receive again in 1933 and 1938.

Double X played six different positions in his career, including pitching, and was not a bad hurler. He took to the mound in 10 games between 1939 and 1945, hurling 23.2 innings that yielded 13 hits, 11 strikeouts, and 14 walks, and posting a most impressive 1.52 ERA and a 1–0 won-lost record.

Many times pitchers did not want to face the powerful three-time World Series hitter, as exemplified in the June 16, 1938, Red Sox game against the Browns—Jimmy was walked six times in succession! The Red Sox won anyway, 12–8.

Foxx was elected to the Hall of Fame in 1951.

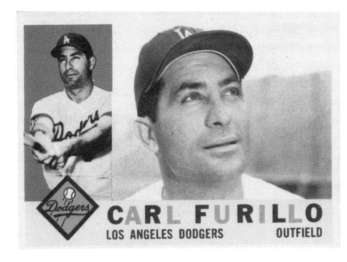

FURILLO, Carl Anthony "Skoonj," "The Reading Rifle"
Born: 3-8-22, Stony Creek Mills, Penna.
Died: 1-21-89, Stony Creek Mills, Penna.
BR   TR   6′   190 lbs.
ESL: Pocomoke City, Md. (1940)
Major Leagues:
    Brooklyn Dodgers (1946–57)
    Los Angeles Dodgers (1958–60)
Position: OF
Career Average: .299

Skoonj appeared in 1,846 major league games, in all as an outfielder for the Dodgers. He had an outstanding 15-year major league career, hitting over .300 on five occasions, and was in seven World Series. In 1953, Furillo won the National League batting title with a .344 average. That same year, he broke his left hand in a fight with Giants manager Leo Durocher.

It was his great throwing arm that earned him his nickname "The Reading Rifle" from a minor league season in Reading, Penna., where he served as a county deputy sheriff.

GLADD, James Walter "Jim"
Born: 10-2-22, Fort Gibson, Okla.
Died: 11-8-77, Long Beach, Calif.
BR   TR   6′2″   190 lbs.
ESL: Milford, Del. (1940)
Major Leagues: New York Giants (1946)
Position: C
Career Average: .091

Gladd played in 84 games for Milford in 1940. He posted a .218 batting average with nine home runs and 32 runs scored. He appeared in four games for the 1946 Giants and went 1 for 11.

GLASS, Thomas Joseph "Tom"
Born: 4-29-98, Greensboro, N.C.
Died: 12-5-81, Greensboro, N.C.
BR   TR   6'3"   170 lbs.
ESL: Cambridge, Md. (1924–25)
Major Leagues: Philadelphia Athletics (1925)
Position: P
Career Record: 1–0

Glass posted a 14–6 won-lost record for Cambridge in 1924 and recorded 107 strike-outs. He had a 10–7 won-lost record during the 1925 season before being promoted to the major leagues. Tom appeared in two games in the majors. He pitched a total of five innings and went out a winner with a career 1–0 won-lost record.

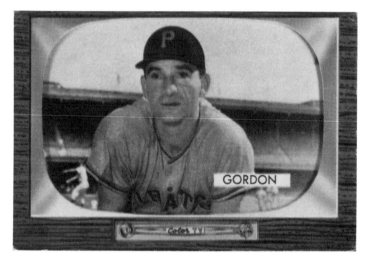

GORDON, Sidney "Sid"
Born: 8-13-17, Brooklyn, N.Y.
Died: 6-17-75, New York, N.Y.
BR   TR   5'10"   185 lbs.
ESL: Milford, Del. (1938)
Major Leagues:
  New York Giants (1941-49)
  Boston Braves (1950–52)
  Milwaukee Braves (1953)
  Pittsburgh Pirates (1954–55)
  New York Giants (1955)
Position: OF
Career Average: .283

Gordon won the Eastern Shore League batting title in 1938 with a .352 average for Milford. In the majors, he hit over 20 home runs in each of five consecutive seasons (1948–52). One of the most popular Giant players ever, he was even given a "night" while with the Giants—before a game played in Brooklyn!

In 1948 Sid hit 30 home runs including three grand slams, and also had 107 RBIs.

In all, he had an outstanding 13-year major league career (not counting the two years he missed while serving in World War II), in which he amassed 202 home runs.

GUERRA, Fermin Romero "Mike"
Born: 10-11-12, Havana, Cuba
Address: 4025 NW 3rd St., Miami, Fla. 33126
BR   TR   5'9"   150 lbs.
ESL: Salisbury, Md. (1937–38)
Major Leagues: Washington Senators (1937–46), Philadelphia Athletics (1947–51),
        Boston Red Sox (1951), Washington Senators (1951)
Position: C
Career Average: .242

Mike Guerra played in 565 major league games. He started with the Senators, playing one game in 1937. That big league debut followed closely his time with the famed Salisbury team of '37 that forfeited 21 wins and then proceeded to win 48 of their final 58 games to capture the ESL pennant and the play-offs.

   Mike hit .281 for the Washington Senators in 1944, and had a .282 average for the A's in 1950. He finished with the Senators in 1951.

HALL, Irvin Gladstone "Irv"
Born: 10-7-18, Alberton, Md.
Address: 1153 Deanwood Rd., Baltimore, Md. 21234
BR   TR   5'10½"   160 lbs.
ESL: Pocomoke City, Md. (1938–39)
Major Leagues: Philadelphia Athletics (1943–46)
Position: 2B/SS
Career Average: .261

Irv led the Eastern Shore League in at bats in 1938, coming to the plate 469 times. He enjoyed his best year in the major leagues at the plate in 1945, when he hit .261 (also his career average) and had 50 RBIs. He played all four infield positions in his major league career.

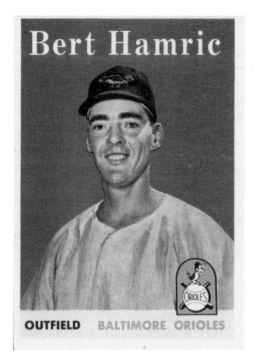

HAMRIC, Odbert Herman "Bert"
Born: 3-1-28, Clarksburg, W.Va.
Died: 8-8-84, Springboro, Ohio
BL   TR   6′   165 lbs.
ESL: Cambridge, Md. (1949)
Major Leagues:
  Brooklyn Dodgers (1955)
  Baltimore Orioles (1958)
Position: OF
Career Average: .111

Bert started in Cambridge as a pitcher, appearing in 27 games, recording a 7–8 record while working 143 innings and posting a 3.45 ERA. He was soon shifted to the outfield, however, because of his batting. After the switch, he played 62 games, hitting .268, and scored 20 runs.

At Newport News in 1951 he hit .304 and led the league in triples. A broken hand kept him from winning the league batting title the following year.

Hamric went 1 for 9 in a total of 10 games in the major leagues. He played in two games for the '55 Dodgers and in eight for the '58 Orioles.

Before he died, he was a shipper for P.H. Glatpelter Co. in West Carrollton, Ohio.

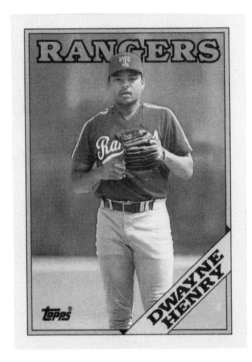

*HENRY, Dwayne Allen
Born: 2-16-62, Elkton, Md.
Address: 502 Hampstead Rd.,
           Middletown, Del. 19709
BR   TR   6′3″   205 lbs.
Major Leagues:
  Texas Rangers 1984–87
Position: P
Career Record: 3–3

Henry was selected by the Texas Rangers in the second round of the free agent draft on June 3, 1980, and reached the major leagues in 1984, when he had a 0–1 record. He split the 1985–87 seasons between Texas and the minor leagues. Dwayne appeared in 19 games for the Rangers in 1986, posting a 1–0 won-lost record. He has suffered injury problems through most of his career.

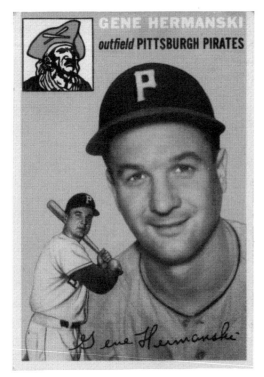

HERMANSKI, Eugene Victor "Gene"
Born: 5-11-20, Pittsfield, Mass.
Address: 100 Hallock Ave., Fox Hall #14,
    Middlesex, N.J. 08846
BL   TR   5′11½″   185 lbs.
ESL: Federalsburg, Md. (1939), Pocomoke
    City, Md. (1940)
Major Leagues:
  Brooklyn Dodgers (1943–50)
  Chicago Cubs (1951–52)
  Pittsburgh Pirates (1953)
Position: OF
Career Average: .272

Gene started his career in the ESL at Federalsburg in 1939, appearing in 10 games and hitting a .196 average. In 1940 he played for Pocomoke City and had a super year, hitting .309 in 121 games, with 133 hits that included 20 doubles, 11 home runs, and 194 total bases.

Hermanski hit .300 his rookie year with the 1943 Dodgers, but then was called to serve in the military until 1946. He played on the Dodger pennant teams of '47 and '49 and appeared in two World Series, playing 11 games. His most consistent major league years were 1948–50 when he hit .290, .299, and .298. He was in 106 games for the Cubs in 1951, batting .273 on the year.

Gene saved Dodger teammate Bobby Morgan from drowning during spring training. He is now a sales representative for Tose Inc. of Fairview, N.J.

116

HOFFERTH, Stewart Edward "Stew"
Born: 1-27-13, Logansport, Ind.
Address: Box 283, Kouts, Ind. 46347
BR   TR   6'2"   195 lbs.
ESL: Cambridge, Md. (1948)
Major Leagues: Boston Braves (1944–46)
Position: C/Manager
Career Average: .216

In three big league seasons with the Braves, Stew caught in 107 games. He hit three home runs and batted .235 in 1945, his best season in the majors.

Stew joined the ESL as player/manager with the Cambridge Dodgers in 1948. He had a fine season as a player that year, appearing in 62 games, with a .335 batting average, including 95 total bases, 19 doubles, and 47 RBIs.

HOHMAN, William Henry
Born: 11-27-03, Baltimore, Md.
Died: 10-29-68, Baltimore, Md.
BR   TR   6'   178 lbs.
ESL: Easton, Md. (1925–26)
Major Leagues: Philadelphia Phillies (1927)
Position: P/OF
Career Average: .278

Bill started with the Easton Farmers in 1925 and, after appearing in 71 games, hitting .282 with seven home runs, was sold to Baltimore. He was sent back to Easton in April 1926 and in 81 games hit .337, with 15 home runs, 18 doubles, and 163 total bases; he was sent up to Baltimore again in August.

Hohman played with Knoxville and Baltimore in 1927 before joining the Phillies. He appeared in seven major league games as an outfielder, going for 18 for the Phillies. He spent the rest of his baseball career in Richmond, New Haven, Springfield, and York before being released in 1932.

HOLBROOK, James Marbury "Sammy"
Born: 7-17-10, Meridian, Miss.
Address: 1215 21st St., Meridian, Miss. 39301
BR   TR   5'11"   189 lbs.
ESL: Federalsburg, Md. (1938–39)
Major Leagues: Washington Senators (1935)
Position: C
Career Average: .259

In one full year (1935) in the big leagues with the Senators, Holbrook caught 47 games with two doubles, two triples, and two home runs. After the Senators let him go following the 1935 season, Sammy wanted to prove to them that they had made a mistake, but was unable to until he reported to Federalsburg in 1938. His first year in the ESL he appeared in 32 games, hitting .361 with 11 doubles and 73 total bases. And Sammy came back in 1939 and had another outstanding year: He hit an excellent .361 in 98 games, which included 110 hits, 17 doubles, 20 home runs, and 191 total bases.

Defensively he led the Eastern Shore League catchers with a .986 fielding percentage and 638 putouts. But Sam still never made it back to the majors.

HONOCHICK, George James "Jim"
Born: 8-19-17, Oneida, Penna.
Address: 10 S. Ott St., Allentown, Penna.
          18104
ESL: 1946
Major Leagues:
   American League (1949–72)
Position: OF/Umpire

Jim is a graduate of Temple University, where he starred in football and baseball. During World War II, he was an ensign in the U.S. Navy and commanded a gun crew.

Jim played in the outfield for the International League Orioles in 1941, 1943, and a portion of 1946 before embarking on an umpiring career. In 1941 he played in 114 games for the Orioles and hit .289 on the season.

He started his professional umpiring career in the Eastern Shore League in 1946, and went up to the International League in 1948. He worked the World Series in 1952 and the all-star game in 1954.

HORSEY, Hanson "Hans"
Born: 11-26-89, Elkton, Md.
Died: 12-1-49, Millington, Md.
ESL: Umpire-in-chief
Major Leagues: Cincinnati Reds (1912)
Position: P
Career Record: 0–0

Hans Horsey was ESL umpire-in-chief for the final four years of the league's existence (1946–49). Ironically, the veteran ump and former major league player died almost exactly when the league folded for the final time.

As a major league pitcher he had his share of problems in the only game he ever pitched in the big time. He hurled four innings, surrendered 14 hits, and left with an ERA of 22.50 for his career. He also went 0 for 2 at the plate.

But he gave the game of baseball 37 years of his life. He got his start at Reading, Penna., in 1910 with the Tri-State League. He was manager of the Jersey City International League team before retiring as an active player in the New York-Penn (new Eastern) League.

Horsey began calling balls and strikes in the original Eastern Shore League in 1925 and later moved up to the Mid-Atlantic League. But when the ESL regrouped in 1937 Horsey came home. He was always a favorite behind the plate with the players, managers, and fans of the ESL.

And he was famous for his quick comebacks to complaints. For example: While Hans was calling a game in Centreville, Md., during the 1946 season, the ever-noisy Dick Waldt was on the mound. "You're having a pretty good night, Hans," Dick said with all the sarcasm he could muster. "You only missed two on that last hitter." Horsey glared at Waldt. "Miss that junk you throw?" he laughed. "Anytime I can't count the stitches on that soft stuff I'll give up. Why, when you pitch I shut one eye to rest it and work the other one." And on a hot Sunday afternoon in Easton, Horsey got off another dilly while working the plate. Midway in the game, he strode back to the grandstand to inform the official scorer of a change in the lineup. A nearby fan asked, "Who's umpiring?" Hans snapped back, "You are, but I'm getting paid for it."

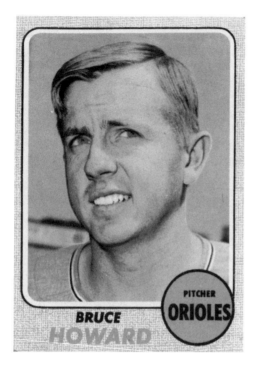

*HOWARD, Bruce Ernest
Born: 3-23-43, Salisbury, Md.
Address: 3114 Bougainvillea, Sarasota,
       Fla. 33579
BB   TR   6'2"   180 lbs.
Major Leagues:
  Chicago White Sox (1963–67)
  Baltimore Orioles (1968)
  Washington Senators (1968)
Position: P
Career Record: 26–31

Howard broke into the majors with the Chicago White Sox in 1963, and had a 2–1 won-lost record with the Chisox in his first two years. He became a regular for the White Sox in 1965 (when he recorded 120 strikeouts), starting 22, 21, and 17 games respectively over the next three seasons. This pitcher was 9–8, 9–5, and 3–10 during that three-year span before splitting the 1968 season between the Baltimore Orioles and the Washington Senators. His best season was 1966, when he posted a 2.30 ERA and had four complete games en route to a 9–5 season.

    Howard stayed in the big leagues for six years, working a total of 528 innings.

HOWELL, Homer Elliott "Dixie"
Born: 4-24-19, Louisville, Ky.
Address: 216 Stonehenge Dr.,
            Louisville, Ky. 40207
BR   TR   5'11½"   190 lbs.
ESL: Dover, Del. (1939)
Major Leagues:
    Pittsburgh Pirates (1947)
    Cincinnati Reds (1949–52)
    Brooklyn Dodgers (1953–56)
Position: C
Career Average: .246

Dixie joined the Eastern Shore League's Dover Club in 1939 and played 86 games, hitting .312 on the year with 20 doubles and 141 total bases.

His best season at bat in the majors was his rookie year with the Pirates, when he hit .276 in 1947. Ironically, he also experimented as a switch-hitter that year.

He caught a total of 315 games in his major league career. Homer "Dixie" Howell is often confused with pitcher Dixie Howell and was in fact a teammate of Millard Fillmore Howell of the 1949 Reds team. He is now on the board of realtors in Kentucky.

HUGHES, Thomas Owen
Born: 10-7-19, Wilkes-Barre, Penna.
Address: RR 4, Mountaintop, Penna. 18707
BR   TR   6'1"   190 lbs.
ESL: Dover, Del. (1939)
Major Leagues: Philadelphia Phillies (1941–47), Cincinnati Reds (1948)
Position: P
Career Record: 31–56

Eastern Shore League fans knew Tommy Hughes was not going to be around Class D ball for long after his 1939 season at Dover: He appeared in 13 games, hurling 80 innings en route to a perfect 9–0 record. He struck out 85 batters in 80 innings and posted a 1.80 ERA.

Hughes compiled a 12–18 won-lost record for the 1942 Phillies with a 3.06 ERA. In his major league career he pitched in 144 games, starting 87. He was 7–3 lifetime as a relief hurler out of the bull pen.

JABLONSKI, Raymond Leo "Jabbo"
Born: 12-17-26, Chicago, Ill.
Died: 11-25-86, Chicago Ill.
BR   TR   5'10"   175 lbs.
ESL: Milford, Del. (1947–48)
Major Leagues:
  St. Louis Cardinals (1953–54)
  Cincinnati Reds (1955–56)
  New York Giants (1957)
  San Francisco Giants (1958)
  St. Louis Cardinals (1959)
  Kansas City Athletics (1960)
Position: 3B
Career Average: .268

Ray came upon the Eastern Shore League scene quietly in 1947, but the following year he and teammate Norm Zauchin put on the greatest one-two batting display in the history of the ESL.

Jabbo in 123 games in 1948 compiled the following statistics: a .354 batting average, 108 runs scored, 172 hits (ESL record), 278 total bases, 24 doubles, 26 home runs, and 131 RBIs.

In his rookie year with the Cardinals he played 157 games with 21 home runs and 112 RBIs in 1953. Sophomore year, he hit .296 with 104 RBIs, and hit .289 for the Giants in 1957. Jabbo played all four infield positions in his major league career but appeared in 630 games at 3B.

FORREST JACOBS
second base PHILA. ATHLETICS

*JACOBS, Forrest Vandergrift "Spook"
Born: 11-4-25, Cheswold, Del.
Address: Box 66, Milford, Del. 19963
BR   TR   5'8½"   155 lbs.
Major Leagues:
   Philadelphia Athletics (1954)
   Kansas City Athletics (1955–56)
   Pittsburgh Pirates (1956)
Position: 2B
Career Average: .247

Jacobs led three different minor leagues in stolen bases: the Mid-Atlantic with 33 in 1947, the Tri-State with 47 in 1948, and the Southern Association with 22 in 1950. He hit .316 for Mobile in 1952.

Spook broke in with the Philadelphia A's in 1954 and collected four hits in his first game in the majors. His rookie year was also his best hitting year at .258 in 132 games with 11 doubles and 63 runs scored. But he lost his regular job at second base after the A's franchise shift to Kansas City and finished his career in 1956 with the Pirates.

One of the smallest players in the major leagues, Spook did not miss a week of baseball in five years, spending his off seasons from the minors playing in the Latin American League every year. He loved the game. Today he owns a donut shop in Milford, Del.

*JOHNSON, William "Judy"
Born: 10-26-99, Snow Hill, Md.
Address: 3701 Kiamensi, Marshalltown, Del. 19808
BR   TR   5'11½"   150 lbs.
Major Leagues: Athletics (1951–54), Phillies (1961–72), Dodgers (1973)
Position: 3B/Manager/Scout

Named by Baseball Writers Association of America Special Committee on Negro
Leagues to the Baseball Hall of Fame in 1975, and called by some baseball experts the
greatest fielding third baseman in the game's history, Judy was before his time and
never had the opportunity to play in the major leagues.

He started his semipro career in Wilmington, Del., in 1918 with the Bacharach club
and played with the Philadelphia All-Stars in 1920. But it was with the famed Hilldale
club of 1921–29 that he earned the respect of all baseball people. He led Hilldale to
three straight titles.

At the tender age of 29 he became manager of the Homestead Grays and later spent
three years with the Pittsburgh Crawfords (1932–35), leading them to a championship
in 1935.

He was a scout for the Athletics 1951–54, Phillies 1961–72, and for the Dodgers in
1973.

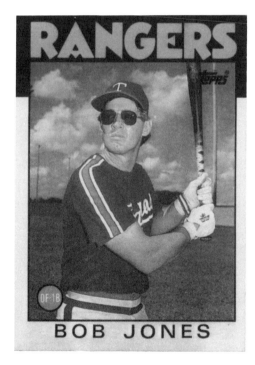

*JONES, Robert Oliver
Born: 10-11-49, Elkton, Md.
Address: 2107 Abeyta Ct., Loveland, Col.
　　　　80537
BL   TL   6'2"   195 lbs.
Major Leagues:
　Texas Rangers (1974–75)
　California Angels (1976–77)
　Texas Rangers (1979–85)
Position: OF
Career Average: .221

124

Jones was selected by the Washington Senators' organization in the thirty-sixth round of the free agent draft in 1967. He played in the minor leagues from 1967 till 1974 before making it up to the major leagues.

This young outfielder spent two years (1976–77) with the California Angels before being signed by the Texas Rangers again in 1979. He tied the major league record for most doubles in an inning (2) on July 2, 1983, while playing with the Rangers. He appeared in 83 games with the Rangers in 1985, and is now manager of the Rangers' minor league team at Port Charlotte.

JORDAN, James William "Jimmy"
Born: 1-13-08, Tucapau, S.C.
Died: 12-4-57, Charlotte, N.C.
BR   TR   5'9"   157 lbs.
ESL: Cambridge, Md. (1925)
Major Leagues: Brooklyn Dodgers (1933–36)
Position: 2B
Career Average: .257

Jimmy Jordan was the regular second baseman for the Cambridge Canners of the 1925 Eastern Shore League. He led the league for second basemen in assists with 285. Appearing in 88 games for the Canners, he hit .228 with 111 total bases.

Jim made it up to the big leagues in 1933 with the Dodgers. He hit .278 for the 1935 Dodgers and was 7 for 21 as a pinch hitter.

KIBLER, J. Thomas "Coach"
Born: 1886, Chestertown, Md.
Died: 10-18-71, Chestertown, Md.
ESL: League President (1937, 1946–47)
Major Leagues: None

Referred to as "Coach" or "Colonel," Kibler started his baseball playing career with the independent Cambridge team of 1908. He moved to coaching and was baseball coach at Lehigh (1909), Ohio State (1910–12), and Washington College (1912–47). He was drafted by the Cincinnati Reds in 1914, but a broken leg ended his baseball playing career. Kibler coached future major leaguers Bill Nicholson, Jake Flowers, Curt Gordy, Johnny Schelberg, Jack Enright, and Dave Leonard. He was inducted into the Maryland Athletic Hall of Fame in 1961.

KOHLMAN, Joseph James "Blackie"
Born: 1-28-13, Philadelphia, Penna.
Died: 3-16-74, Philadelphia, Penna.
BR   TR   6'   160 lbs.
ESL: Salisbury, Md. (1937)
Major Leagues: Washington Senators (1937–38)
Position: P
Career Record: 1–0

In his two years with the Senators Blackie appeared in nine games (two starts) and compiled a career 1–0 record.

His ESL experience, however, was what drew plaudits. Topping off that famous minor league season that won his manager (Jake Flowers) the *Sporting News* Minor League Manager of the Year Award, Kohlman hurled a no-hitter in the deciding game of the league play-offs. He led the ESL in strikeouts in 1937 with 257, and was also the ESL leader in complete games, with 23 that season. Finally, Kohlman holds the all-time minor league record for winning percentage (25 credit games) at .962 for his 25–1 mark in 1937.

KRAUSSE, Louis Bernard, Sr. "Lew"
Born: 6-8-12, Media, Penna.
Address: 3680 Edgerton Circle, Sarasota, Fla. 33581
BR   TR   6'1/2"   167 lbs.
ESL: Federalsburg, Md. (1946)
Major Leagues: Philadelphia Athletics (1931–32)
Position: P
Career Record: 5–1

Krausse broke into the major leagues as a 19-year-old with the Philadelphia Athletics. He appeared in 20 games in 1932, compiling a 4–1 record (including one shutout); started three games (two completed); and had a 2–1 relief record.

So Lew Krausse, Sr., was a 34-year-old seasoned baseball veteran when he came to the Eastern Shore League in 1946. It didn't seem to bother him, however, as he appeared in 29 games, posting an 11–12 record with 216 innings pitched and a 4.25 ERA. He led the league in innings pitched and tied with Mike Gast of Centreville with 21 complete games.

Lew is the father of major leaguer Lew Krausse, Jr.

LEVEY, James Julius "Jim"
Born: 9-13-06, Pittsburgh, Penna.
Died: 3-14-70, Dallas, Tex.
BR   TR   5'10½"   154 lbs.
ESL: Salisbury, Md. (1927)
Major Leagues: St. Louis Browns (1930–33)
Position: SS
Career Average: .230

Jim's best year at the plate in the major leagues was 1932 when he became a switch-hitter and batted .280 with 30 doubles. He played 437 games at shortstop in his big league career.

LUCAS, Frederick Warrington "Fritz"
Born: 1-19-03, Vineland, N.J.
Died: 1986, Cambridge, Md.
BR   TR   5'10"   165 lbs.
ESL: Cambridge, Md. (1937, '39)
Major Leagues: Philadelphia Phillies (1935)
Position: OF/Manager/President of the League (1949)
Career Average: .265

It is a strange coincidence that Fred Lucas lived and died in the house where I was born and spent the first 12 years of my life.

Fritz started his baseball career in 1923 at Martinsburg of the Blue Ridge League. In 1929 at Charleroi, Penna., of the Mid-Atlantic League he rewrote the record books: He hit .407 with 178 hits, 113 RBIs, 21 home runs, and 24 doubles—all single season league records. In the major leagues as a player in 1935, he got into 20 games and went 9 for 34.

"Mr. Baseball" to most all of Dorchester County, Fred was sent to Cambridge in 1937 as player/manager of the Cambridge Cardinals. He appeared in 29 games as a player and hit .309 on the year.

After starting a managing career in Cambridge Lucas later went on to manage Hamilton, Ont., and Union Springs of the Georgia-Alabama League. He joined the Brooklyn Dodger organization and helped revive the ESL in 1946 as business manager of the Cambridge Dodgers and later was president of the ESL.

Fritz retired after over 30 years in politics following his baseball career.

LYNN, Jerome Edward "Jerry"
Born: 4-20-16, Scranton, Penna.
Died: 9-25-72, Scranton, Penna.
BR   TR   5'10"   164 lbs.
ESL: Salisbury, Md. (1937)
Major Leagues: Washington Senators (1937)
Position: 2B
Career Average: .667

Jerry was one of several members of the 1937 pennant-winning Salisbury club of the ESL to make the Senators at the end of the season. He led the Eastern Shore League in batting in '37, hitting .342, and was then sold to Washington. Jerry played in one game for the 1937 Senators at the end of the season and went 2 for 3 including a double. That was the start and finish of his major league career.

MACK, Cornelius Alexander "Connie"
Born: 2-22-62, E. Brookfield, Mass.
Died: 2-8-56, Philadelphia, Penna.
BR   TR   6'1"   150 lbs.
ESL: Federalsburg, Md. (1947)
Major Leagues: Washington Senators (1886–89), Buffalo Bisons (1890), Pittsburgh
          Pirates (1891–96), Philadelphia Athletics (1901–50)
Position: Player/Manager/President

Connie Mack managed longer (53 years) than anyone in the history of major league baseball. His teams won nine American League pennants and five world championships. He never smoked, cursed, or drank heavily.

    While still the manager of the Philadelphia A's he served as president of the Federalsburg A's with son Earle as general manager.

MACK, Earle Thaddeus
Born: 2-1-89, Spencer, Mass.
Died: 2-5-67, Upper Darby, Penna.
BR   TR   5'7"   164 lbs.
ESL: Federalsburg, Md. (1947)
Major Leagues: Philadelphia Athletics (1910–14)
Position: IF/C/Vice-President
Career Average: .125

When Earle's father Connie Mack became president of the Federalsburg Baseball Club in 1947, he named Earle vice-president. Earle had played for three seasons in the major leagues, appearing in a total of five games, going 2 for 16 at the plate. His career totals were a .125 batting average with one triple and one RBI.

MAIER, Robert Phillip "Bob"
Born: 9-5-15, Dunellen, N.J.
Address: 334 Dunellen Ave., Dunellen, N.J. 08812
BR   TR   5'8"   180 lbs.
ESL: Salisbury, Md. (1938–39)
Major Leagues: Detroit Tigers (1945)
Position: 3B
Career Average: .263

Bob went 1 for 1 in the 1945 World Series. He hit .263 and had 34 RBIs as the Tigers' regular third baseman in 1945.

MALZONE, Frank James
Born: 2-28-30, Bronx, N.Y.
Address: 16 Aletha Rd.,
              Needham, Mass. 02192
BR   TR   5'10"   180 lbs.
ESL: Milford, Del. (1948)
Major Leagues:
  Boston Red Sox (1955–65)
  California Angels (1966)
Position: 3B

Milford teammates Ray Jablonski and Norm Zauchin stole much of Malzone's thunder in 1948, but he still logged a respectable year at bat in the ESL—he had a .304 average, with 32 doubles and 107 runs.

In his major league debut, September 20, 1955, against the Orioles, Frank went 6 for 10 in a doubleheader. Altogether, Frank played third base (never any other position) in 1,370 major league games. He led the American League in double plays from 1957 through 1961, and was voted all-time Red Sox third baseman in 1969.

Mr. Consistency had an average of 15 to 20 home runs and 80 to 90 RBIs over his career, and a .274 lifetime batting average. He also had 239 doubles in his career, with over 30 in each of four seasons.

Malzone is now a scout for the Boston Red Sox.

129

MARKELL, Harry Duquesne "Duke"
Born: 8-17-23, Paris, France
Died: 7-26-84, Palm Beach, Fla.
BR   TR   6'1½"   209 lbs.
ESL: Seaford, Del. (1946–47)
Major Leagues: St. Louis Browns (1951)
Position: P
Career Record: 1–1

Duke played in the Eastern Shore League under his real name of Makowsky. He got off to a good start in the 1946 ESL, appearing in 13 games for Seaford, and (although recording only a 5–5 won-lost record) was second in the league with a 1.59 ERA.

Duke came back in 1947 to tie Cambridge's Chris Van Cuyk for most complete games (24) and led the league in innings pitched (249). He logged a 19–9 record in '47.

He pitched five games for the 1951 Browns, and was also a New York City policeman while he played professional baseball.

MARNIE, Harry Sylvester "Hal"
Born: 7-6-18, Philadelphia, Penna.
Address: 2715 S. Smetley, Philadelphia, Penna. 19145
BR   TR   6'1"   178 lbs.
ESL: Crisfield, Md. (1937), Centreville, Md. (1938)
Major Leagues: Philadelphia Phillies (1940–42)
Position: 3B
Career Average: .221

Hal broke in with the Crisfield Crabbers of the ESL in 1937, playing in 82 games at third base and hitting .238 on the year. He was traded to Centreville of the ESL the following year, where he hit .263 in 112 games, with 81 runs scored, and had 118 hits, including 20 doubles.

Hal was converted to a second baseman in the majors but still filled in at both third base and shortstop for the Phils. His best year in the major leagues was 1941 when he hit .241 for the Phillies, playing in 61 games. He also scored 12 runs and had 11 RBIs that season.

MARSHALL, Charles Anthony
Born: 8-28-19, Wilmington, Del.
Address: 1 Radcliff Court, Wilmington, Del. 19804
BR   TR   5'10½"   178 lbs.
ESL: Cambridge, Md. (1937–38)
Major Leagues: St. Louis Cardinals (1941)
Position: C
Career Average: .000

Born Charles Anthony Marczlewicz, Charlie led the Eastern Shore League catchers in assists in 1937 with 56, appearing in 88 games for the Cambridge Cardinals, hitting .246 on the year. He came back in 1938 to lead the ESL catchers with a .993 fielding percentage. He also improved with the bat, hitting .248 with 106 total bases and six home runs.

Charlie got into one game in the major leagues with the 1941 Cardinals as a catcher but never got a time to bat.

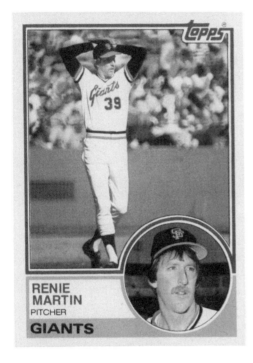

*MARTIN, Donald Renie
Born: 8-30-55, Dover, Del.
Address: Fairview Ave., Dover, Del. 19901
BR   TR   6'4"   190 lbs.
Major Leagues:
  Kansas City Royals (1979–81)
  San Francisco Giants (1982–84)
  Philadelphia Phillies (1984)
Position: P
Career Record: 24–35

Martin was selected by the Kansas City Royals in the nineteenth round of the June 1977 free agent draft. He was 6–2 at Omaha when called up to Kansas City in 1979. Renie had five saves for the Royals—second best on the team despite having only played with the club less than two months.

In 1980 Martin made his first big league start on May 10 and beat the Red Sox 13–8, was 10–10 for the year with 20 starts, and appeared in three World Series games.

The 26-year-old pitcher was traded to San Francisco in 1981 when he logged a 4–5 overall record, and was 7–10 with the Giants in 1982 and 2–4 in 1983.

He holds a B.S. degree in finance from the University of Richmond.

MATTIS, Ralph L.
Born: 8-24-90, Roxborough, Penna.
Died: 9-13-60, Williamsport, Penna.
BR   TR   5'11"   172 lbs.
ESL: Crisfield, Md. (1925)
Major Leagues: Pittsburgh Pirates (1914)
Position: OF
Career Average: .247

Ralph displayed his veteran ability in the ESL in 1925 by playing in 90 games and hitting .311. He scored 66 runs, and had 109 hits including 23 home runs and 197 total bases.

  Mattis played with Pittsburgh in the Federal League. He appeared in 36 games, going 21 for 85 at the plate.

MICELOTTA, Robert Peter "Mickey"
Born: 10-20-28, Corona, N.Y.
Address: 295 Saville Rd., Mineola, N.Y.
         11501
BR   TR   5'11"   185 lbs.
ESL: Dover, Del. (1948)
Major Leagues:
  Philadelphia Phillies (1954–55)
Position: SS
Career Average: .000

Mickey broke into organized baseball in 1947 with Carbondale. He had a good year in 1949 (following his Eastern Shore League year at Dover) when he hit .286 with 87 RBIs at Vandergrift. Micelotta spent the 1950 season at Schenectady of the Eastern League, and then went into the army for 1951 and 1952. The two-year interruption caused by his military service was felt by many in the game to have cost him a long major league career.

Mick spent five years in the minor leagues, with his best season coming at Terre Haute of the Three I League in 1953. Moving up to the Phillies, he appeared in 17 major league games without getting a base hit; he was 0 for 7 at the plate, but did score two runs as a pinch runner.

A little idiosyncrasy of Mickey's was that although he had normal vision, he would wear glasses when playing. Micelotta now works for the Hudson Carpet Company, Bronx, N. Y.

MILLER, Stuart Leonard "Stu"
Born: 12-26-27, Northampton, Mass.
Address: 252 Devonshire Blvd., San
        Carlos, Calif. 94070
BR   TR   5'11½"   165 lbs.
ESL: Salisbury, Md. (1949)
Major Leagues:
  St. Louis Cardinals (1952–56)
  Philadelphia Phillies (1956)
  New York Giants (1957)
  San Francisco Giants (1958–62)
  Baltimore Orioles (1963–67)
  Atlanta Braves (1968)
Position: P
Career Record: 105–103

One of the top firemen in major league history, Stu played for Salisbury of the ESL in 1949 and appeared in 29 games, posting an unimpressive 8–13 mark while hurling 151 innings with eight complete games and a 4.29 ERA. Still ahead of him, however, was a bright major league career.

Stu pitched a shutout in his major league debut. He led the National League with a 2.47 ERA in 1958, and won 14 games and had 17 saves for the 1961 Giants. He was

National League Fireman of the Year in 1961 and American League Fireman of the Year in 1963, the only pitcher to win the award in both leagues.

Miller had 27 saves for the 1963 Orioles and had 154 saves in his career. His career record as a relief pitcher was 79–67.

Stu had been the winning pitcher in the 1961 all-star game at Candlestick Park and thus it was appropriate to honor him by having him throw out the first ball at the 1984 all-star game in the same park.

MILLIES, Walter Louis "Wally"
Born: 10-18-06, Chicago, Ill.
Address: 5312 W. 96th St., Oak Lawn, Ill. 60453
BR   TR   5'10½"   170 lbs.
ESL: Dover, Del. (1938), Milford, Del. (1946–47)
Major Leagues: Brooklyn Dodgers (1934), Washington Senators (1936–37), Philadelphia
                Phillies (1939–41)
Position: C/Manager
Career Average: .243

Wally hit .312 for the 1936 Washington Senators and scored 26 runs with 25 RBIs. He also had 28 RBIs the following year but hit only .223 on the year. After those two seasons in the major leagues Walt was sent down to the Dover club of the Eastern Shore League in 1938 where he appeared in 49 games, hitting .333 in the process.

He went back up to the majors in 1939 but once more returned to the ESL in 1946–47—but this time as player/manager of the Milford club. During the 1946 season he hit .353 in 40 games and stuck to managing the club in 1947.

Wallie caught 239 games in his major league career. He is now a scout for the Montreal Expos.

MOFORD, Herbert
Born: 8-6-28, Brooksville, Ky.
Address: P.O. Box 12, Minerva, Ky. 41062
BR   TR   6'1"   175 lbs.
ESL: Salisbury, Md. (1947–48)
Major Leagues:
  St. Louis Cardinals (1955)
  Detroit Tigers (1958)
  Boston Red Sox (1959)
  New York Mets (1962)
Position: P
Career Record: 5–13

Moford came to the Eastern Shore League with Salisbury in 1947 and appeared in 18 games, posting a 5–9 record with a 3.86 ERA. In 1948 he came back to the Redbirds and showed his stuff by fashioning a 20–4 won-lost record with a league-leading six shutouts. That same year he had a 2.39 ERA, completing 19 of 26 starts, and pitched 207 innings, striking out 129 batters.

Moford played for four major league teams in 50 games over the seven-year span of his majors career. His most productive season was in 1958 when he was 4–9 for the Tigers. He started 11 games that year and completed six.

Today Herb is farming in his native Kentucky.

MONCHAK, Alex
Born: 3-5-17, Bayonne, N.J.
Address: 7414 8th Ave., West Bradenton, Fla. 34209
BR   TR   6'   180 lbs.
ESL: Dover, Del. (1938–39)
Major Leagues: Philadelphia Phillies (1940)
Position: SS
Career Average: .143

Alex fashioned two great years in the ESL for Dover. He hit .303 in 95 games the first season, with 86 runs scored, 118 hits, 10 home runs, and 183 total bases. He came back in 1939 to top all categories, hitting .337 in 104 games, with 88 runs scored, 131 hits, 15 home runs, 210 total bases, and 73 RBIs.

Monchak appeared in 19 games for the 1940 Phillies and went 2 for 14.

He has been active in baseball from 1937 up to the present, except for a hiatus 1943–45 while he was in military service. He managed in the minor leagues from 1949 to 1961; was a scout and farm system instructor for the California Angels 1962–79; coached the Chicago White Sox 1971–75; coached the Oakland Athletics in 1976; and coached for Pittsburgh and Atlanta until 1988.

*MORRIS, John Wallace
Born: 8-23-41, Lewes, Del.
Address: 5538 Paradise Ln., Scottsdale,
      Ariz. 85254
BR   TL   6'2"   195 lbs.
Major Leagues:
  Philadelphia Phillies (1966)
  Baltimore Orioles (1968)
  Seattle Mariners (1969)
  Milwaukee Brewers (1970–71)
  San Francisco Giants (1972–74)
Position: P
Career Record: 11–7

John spent six years toiling in the minors and missed all of 1963 due to an injury. He made his major league debut with the Phillies in 1966. He was primarily a relief pitcher for his entire career, although he did start nine games for Milwaukee in 1970 en route to a 4–3 record.

Morris was 2–0 with the Orioles in 1968, appearing in 19 games with a 2.56 ERA. In addition to the Phillies, Brewers, and Orioles, he also hurled for Seattle one season (1969), and ended his major league career with the San Francisco Giants (1972–74).

MOSS, Charles Crosby "Charlie"
Born: 3-20-11, Meridian, Miss.
Address: 2400 40th St., Meridian, Miss. 39304
BR   TR   5'10"   160 lbs.
ESL: Federalsburg, Md. (1938)
Major Leagues: Philadelphia Athletics (1934–36)
Position: C
Career Average: .246

Charlie came to Federalsburg of the ESL and appeared in 17 games, hitting .340 during his stay. He had spent three years with the major leagues, appearing in 47 games for Philadelphia. He caught 26 games and was 4 for 20 as a pinch hitter. His best year was 1936, when he appeared in 33 games, hitting .250 and going 11 for 44.

MUICH, Ignatius Andrew "Joe"
Born: 11-23-03, St. Louis, Mo.
Address: 9244 Lodge Pole Lane, St. Louis, Mo. 63126
BR   TR   6'2"   175 lbs.
ESL: Dover, Del. (1924)
Major Leagues: Boston Nationals (1924)
Position: P
Career Record: 0–0

Joe Muich started the 1924 Eastern Shore League season at Dover and pitched 92 innings, logging a 5–5 won-lost record.

He was called up to the Boston Nationals at the end of the ESL season (which ran from May 30 till September 1).

In his brief major league career he appeared in three games for the Nationals, hurling nine innings yielding 19 hits with an 11.00 ERA. Joe was also 0 for 3 at the plate.

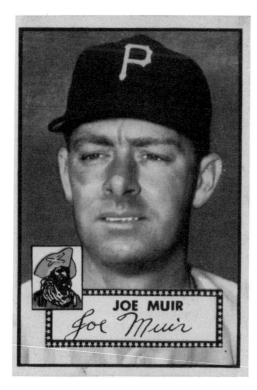

MUIR, Joseph Allen "Joe"
Born: 11-26-22, Oriole, Md.
Died: 6-25-80, Baltimore, Md.
BL   TL   6'1"   172 lbs.
ESL: Rehoboth Beach, Del. (1947)
Major Leagues:
  Pittsburgh Pirates (1951–52)
Position: P
Career Record: 2–5

Joe got a late start in professional baseball after serving 2½ years in the Marine Corps, making his pro debut in 1947 with Rehoboth Beach of the ESL. It was an impressive start. Joe was third best hurler in the ESL that year with a 2.94 ERA. He appeared in 22 games, completing 16 and logging 134 strikeouts. Not bad with the bat either, he led the league in pinch-hitting with a .333 average.

Muir went up to Indianapolis where he posted a 19–18 mark. He had an overall minor league career record of 51–34.

In 1951 he was 0–2 for the Pirates, although he had a respectable 2.76 ERA. Joe appeared in 12 games for the 1952 Bucs, compiling a 2–3 record. He had an overall minor league career record of 51–34.

After retirement from professional baseball Joe entered the Maryland State Police and rose to the rank of sergeant before retiring.

MULLIGAN, Richard Charles "Dick"
Born: 3-18-18, Wilkes-Barre, Penna.
Address: 1205 E. Walnut Ave., Victoria, Tex. 77901
BL   TL   6'   167 lbs.
ESL: Federalsburg, Md. (1940)
Major Leagues: Washington Senators (1941), Philadelphia Phillies (1946), Boston Braves
                (1946–47)
Position: P
Career Record: 3–3

Dick worked in 29 games, hurling 196 innings for Federalsburg in 1940. He completed
20 games that year, etching a 16–8 won-lost record with 164 strikeouts and a 2.25 ERA.
   Dick appeared in 23 games with the Phillies and Braves in 1946, compiling a 3–2
won-lost record, and was 1–0 in relief.

MURRAY, Joseph Ambrose
Born: 11-11-20, Wilkes-Barre, Penna.
Address: 2719 Via Santa Tomas, San Clemente, Calif. 92672
BL   TL   6'   165 lbs.
ESL: Easton, Md. (1940–41)
Major Leagues: Philadelphia Athletics (1950)
Position: P
Career Record: 0–3

Joe saw action in 27 games with Easton in 1940 with 10 complete games as he posted a
6–14 record. He worked 128 innings for a 3.52 ERA. He came back to the ESL's Easton
team in 1941 to hurl in 33 games with a 13–8 record and a 3.13 ERA. The
twenty-one-year-old pitched 144 innings, striking out 140.
   Joe appeared in eight games for the 1950 Athletics in his major league career. He is
now a roofer in San Clemente.

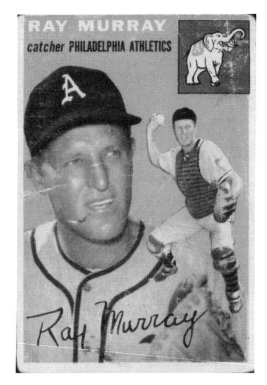

MURRAY, Raymond Lee "Deacon"
Born: 10-12-17, Spring Hope, N.C.
Address: Box 453, Kennedale, Tex. 76060
BR   TR   6'3"   204 lbs.
ESL: Pocomoke City, Md. (1940)
Major Leagues:
  Cleveland Indians (1948–50)
  Philadelphia Athletics (1951–53)
  Baltimore Orioles (1954)
Position: C
Career Average: .252

Ray caught in 90 games for the 1940 Pocomoke City club, hitting .263 with 100 total bases. He was not one to give up on making it to the major leagues and was 30 years old when he finally made it.

Deacon hit .284 for the 1953 A's with 14 doubles and 41 RBIs. A better hitter at night than day, he proved it by hitting .330 under the lights for the Athletics in 1953. Deacon caught 226 games in the major leagues.

Once he had a disagreement with an umpire while he was catching. He decided not to start an argument and risk being thrown out of game so he politely turned and handed the ump a card that read, "Time to See Your Eye Doctor. Dr. Smith, Palm Beach, Florida."

Ray is now a county sheriff in Fort Worth, Tex.

MURTAUGH, Daniel Edward "Danny"
Born: 10-8-17, Chester, Penna.
Died: 12-2-76, Chester, Penna.
BR   TR   5'9"   165 lbs.
ESL: Cambridge, Md. (1937–38)
Major Leagues:
    Philadelphia Phillies (1941–46)
    Boston Braves (1947)
    Pittsburgh Pirates (1948–51)
Position: 2B
Career Average: .254

Danny came to Cambridge in 1937 and played in 94 games, collecting 112 hits for a .297 average. The following year he appeared in 112 games, hitting .312, with 134 hits, 21 doubles, and 174 total bases. Dan also led the ESL in sacrifices (13) in 1938. Later he led the Texas League with 106 runs scored in 1940.

He was called up to the major leagues in midseason 1941 with the Phillies and still managed to lead the National League in stolen bases with 18. In 1946 in the International League he tied the league lead with 174 hits. Two years later, in 1948, Danny led the National League's second basemen in putouts, assists, and fielding chances with the Pirates. That same year he hit .290. In 1950 his average with the Bucs was .294.

Murtaugh, a generous man, always credited Fred Lucas of Cambridge for his baseball success.

NAPP, Larry Albert
Born: 5-21-19, Brooklyn, N.Y.
Address: 200 NW Bel Air Dr., Ft.
       Lauderdale, Fla. 33313
ESL: 1938
Major Leagues:
  American League
Position: Umpire (1951–72)

Larry Napp came to Pocomoke City of the Eastern Shore League as a catcher-outfielder in 1938 but appeared in fewer than 10 games. He moved up to the PONY (Pennsylvania-Ontario, Canada-New York) League in 1939 and to the Michigan State League in 1940.

Larry began his umpiring career with the Mid-Atlantic League in 1948, and worked the World Series in 1954.

Larry was also licensed to referee for the New York State boxing commission. He is now assistant supervisor of umpires for the American League.

NICHOLAS, Donald Leigh "Little Nick"
Born: 10-30-30, Phoenix, Ariz.
Address: 12311 Chase, Garden Grove, Calif. 92645
BL   TR   5'7"   150 lbs.
ESL: Cambridge, Md. (1948)
Major Leagues: Chicago White Sox (1952–54)
Position: OF
Career Average: .000

At the age of 17, Little Nick came to Cambridge of the ESL in midseason and still managed to draw 130 bases on balls (three short of the league record). His ability to steal bases—he stole six in a game on September 2, 1948, against the Rehoboth Beach Pirates at Dodger Park—made him a favorite of the Cambridge Dodger fans. He holds the ESL record for stolen bases, with 82 to his credit.

In his majors career, he had only two plate appearances in two years, although he did manage to score three runs. He was a pinch hitter and runner for the White Sox in 10 games in 1952 and 1954. During the off season Nicholas was a medical student at the University of Arizona.

NICHOLS, Roy
Born: 3-3-21, Little Rock, Ark.
Address: 104 Arias Way, Hot Springs Village, Ark. 71901
BR   TR   5'11"   155 lbs.
ESL: Cambridge, Md. (1947)
Major Leagues: New York Giants (1944)
Position: 3B/Manager
Career Average: .222

Roy Nichols made a smart impression on Cambridge Dodger fans of the ESL in 1947 when he led them to the league pennant. As a player on that championship team he hit .355 (second in league), had 133 RBIs (tied for league lead), and led the league with 35 doubles. Roy was named to the all-star slugging team that year.

In his only major league season he went 2 for 9 at the plate in 11 games for the New York Giants.

*NICHOLSON, William Beck "Swish"
Born: 12-11-14, Chestertown, Md.
Address: RR 3, Chestertown, Md. 21620
BL   TR   6'   205 lbs.
Major Leagues:
   Philadelphia Athletics (1936)
   Chicago Cubs (1939–48)
   Philadelphia Phillies (1949–53)
Position: OF
Career Average: .268

A graduate of Washington College, Swish spent 16 years in the major leagues and appeared in one World Series and four all-star games.

He led the National League in 1943 with 29 home runs and 128 RBIs. The next year was even better: On July 22 and 23, he hit four consecutive home runs. For all of 1944 he hit .287 with a league-leading 33 home runs, 116 runs scored, and 122 RBIs. He missed winning the National League's MVP award with the Cubs by one vote to Marty Marion.

In 1949 he was traded from the Cubs to the Phillies, with whom he played as utility outfielder and pinch hitter. On Labor Day in 1950 he learned he was suffering from diabetes, and missed the rest of the season. He is now a retired tobacco farmer living on his farm outside of Chestertown.

NORTHEY, Ronald James "The Round Man"
Born: 4-26-20, Mahanoy City, Penna.
Died: 4-16-71, Pittsburgh, Penna.
BL   TR   5'10"   195 lbs.
ESL: Federalsburg, Md. (1939)
Major Leagues:
    Philadelphia Phillies (1942–47)
    St. Louis Cardinals (1947–49)
    Cincinnati Reds (1950)
    Chicago Cubs (1950–52)
    Chicago White Sox (1955–57)
    Philadelphia Phillies (1957)
Position: OF
Career Average: .276

Eastern Shore League fans knew Ron Northey would not be in Class D ball for long when in 1939 with Federalsburg he appeared in 79 games, hitting .343, with 110 hits, 23 doubles, 23 home runs, 70 RBIs, and 214 total bases.

Northey's best hitting years were 1943 (.278), 1944 (.288), 1947 (.288), 1948 (.321), and 1950 (.272). Then he became a pinch hitter extraordinaire:

He established a major league career record (since equalled) of three pinch-hit, grand-slam home runs. The Round Man led the American League in pinch hits in 1956 with 15 for the White Sox, and on July 10, 1957, tied a major league record with a ninth pinch-hit home run.

At the end of his career Northey coached with the Pirates.

OSTROWSKI, Joseph Paul "Professor"
Born: 11-15-16, W. Wyoming, Penna.
Address: 441 Tripp St., W. Wyoming,
      Penna. 18644
BL   TL   6'   180 lbs.
ESL: Centreville, Md. (1941)
Major Leagues:
  St. Louis Browns (1948–49)
  New York Yankees (1950–52)
Position: P
Career Record: 23–25

Joe topped the ESL with a sparkling 1.71 ERA in 1941, while posting a 10–4 record, appearing in 17 games for 126 innings. He had 74 strikeouts.

Like many another, his career was interrupted by World War II. However, when he returned, it was to the major leagues. Ostrowski played with three American League pennant teams and one World Series championship Yankee team. He was the ace of the Yankee relief corps in 1951 when he worked more games than any other Yankee except Allie Reynolds. Also in 1951, he was 4 and 4 with five saves as relief ace.

The Professor graduated from Scranton University and taught school during the off season. He also worked as a basketball referee. He is now retired and lives in the town of his birth.

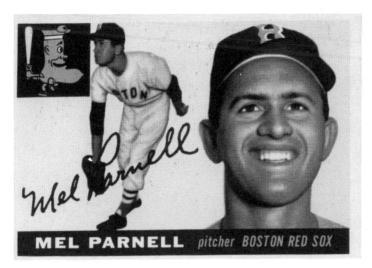

MEL PARNELL   pitcher BOSTON RED SOX

PARNELL, Melvin Lloyd "Dusty"
Born: 6-13-22, New Orleans, La.
Address: 700 Turquoise St., New Orlean.
     La. 70124
BL   TL   6′   180 lbs.
ESL: Centreville, Md. (1941)
Major Leagues:
  Boston Red Sox (1947–56)
Position: P
Career Record: 123–75

Unlike that of his 1941 pitching teammate Joe Ostrowski, Parnell's ESL year was not spectacular—he saved his best for the major leagues.

In his early majors career, Mel led the American League in 1949 with a 25–7 won-lost record, a 2.77 ERA, and 295 innings pitched. He won 21 games in 1953, including shutting out the Yankees four times. But he went into the baseball record books on July 14, 1956, when he hurled a no-hitter at Fenway Park against the White Sox.

Opposing players also feared Dusty as a batter in the days before there were designated hitters—he hit over .300 on two occasions. Favorite victims (as well as the Yankees) were the Tigers, Athletics, and Senators, with a 66–19 mark over the latter through 1956.

A humorous anecdote concerned the time he slept through a game in 1955 because he thought a night game was scheduled. Today Mel is owner of Parnell and Tullier Pest Control Services in New Orleans.

PELEKOUDAS, Chris G.
Born: 1-23-18, Chicago, Ill.
Died: 11-30-84, Sunnyvale, Calif.
ESL: 1948
Major Leagues: National League (1960–72)
Position: Umpire

146

PENNOCK, Herbert Jefferis
Born: 2-10-94, Kennett Square, Penna.
Died: 1-30-48, New York, N.Y.
BB   TL   6′   160 lbs.
ESL: Dover, Del. (1947)
Position: Vice-President
Major Leagues: Philadelphia Athletics (1912–15), Boston Red Sox (1915–22), New York
          Yankees (1923–33), Boston Red Sox (1934)
Position: P
Career Record: 240–162

Pennock was in the major leagues for 22 years and compiled a 240–162 record. He led the American League in winning percentages in 1923 while with the Yankees with a .760 mark. He also led the American League in innings pitched in 1925 with 277. Pennock was undefeated in five World Series (5–0) appearances. He pitched in 617 games in his career, working 3,558 innings.

Pennock came to the ESL with the Dover Phillies as the club's V.P.

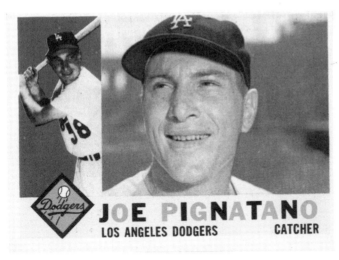

JOE PIGNATANO
LOS ANGELES DODGERS   CATCHER

PIGNATANO, Joseph Benjamin
Born: 8-4-29, Brooklyn, N.Y.
Address: 150 78th St., Brooklyn,
          N. Y. 11209
BR   TR   5′10″   180 lbs.
ESL: Cambridge, Md. (1949)
Major Leagues:
  Brooklyn Dodgers (1957)
  Los Angeles Dodgers (1958–60)
  Kansas City Athletics (1961)
  San Francisco Giants (1962)
  New York Mets (1962)
Position: C
Career Average: .234

Joe broke into the Eastern Shore League with the Cambridge Dodgers in the final year of the league operation in 1949, appearing in 87 games and hitting .233 on the season.

In 1953 Joe led the Tri-State League in triples! Who said catchers are slow?

He filled in for Roy Campanella when the Dodger catcher was injured. Pignatano played in one World Series without making a plate appearance, and played 3B in two games for the 1961 Athletics. Joe ended his major league career in 1962 against the Cubs by hitting into a triple play.

He is now a coach for the Atlanta Braves, joining Don Zimmer (Cubs) as the only remaining former ESL players on active major league rosters.

PITKO, Alex "Spunk"
Born: 11-22-14, Burlington, N.J.
Address: 8001 E. Broadway, Mesa, Ariz. 85208
BR   TR   5'10"   160 lbs.
ESL: Centreville, Md. (1937)
Major Leagues: Philadelphia Phillies (1938), Washington Senators (1939)
Position: OF
Career Average: .259

Alex had a great year with the Centreville Colts in 1937, hitting .328 on the season. He led the ESL in runs scored (103), triples (8), and home runs (20) that year.

Pitko jumped from the ESL to the major leagues in 1938. He appeared in 11 games in the major leagues during the 1938–39 seasons, going 7 for 27.

POHOLSKY, Thomas George
Born: 8-6-29, Detroit, Mich.
Address: 177 Horseshoe Dr., Kirkwood,
                Mo. 63122
BR   TR   6'3"   205 lbs.
ESL: Milford, Del. (1946)
Major Leagues:
    St. Louis Cardinals (1950–56)
    Chicago Cubs (1957)
Position: P
Career Record: 31–52

Poholsky broke into professional baseball in 1945 before being assigned to Milford of the Eastern Shore League in 1946. He went to the International League where he led in total wins and ERA in 1950. He was also voted Most Valuable Player of the league that year. In a 1950 game he pitched all 22 innings in a 2-1 win.

Poholsky appeared in 159 games in major leagues (starting 104 with 30 complete games), but was never able to post a winning won-lost record in big leagues, his closest being in 1955 when he was 9-11.

He is a graduate of Washington University in St. Louis with a degree in civil engineering.

POLAND, Hugh Reid
Born: 1-19-13, Tompkinsville, Ky.
Died: 3-30-84, Guthrie, Ky.
BL   TR   5'11½"   185 lbs.
ESL: Cambridge, Md. (1940)
Major Leagues: New York Giants (1943), Boston Braves (1943–47), Philadelphia Phillies
                (1947), Cincinnati Reds (1947–48)
Position: C
Career Average: .185

Hugh had an outstanding ESL season with Cambridge in 1940, playing in 88 games and hitting .310 with 95 hits, 14 doubles, and 140 total bases. He also led the ESL catchers in assists (64) and putouts (588).

In the majors Poland was 4 for 14 as a pinch hitter for the 1947 Reds and hit .231 overall that season, which he split between the Phillies and the Reds. He caught a total of 55 games in the major leagues.

POPOWSKI, Edward Joseph "Pop"
Born: 8-20-13, Sayreville, N.J.
Address: P.O. Box 45, Sayreville, N.J. 08872
ESL: Centreville, Md. (1941)
Major Leagues: Boston Red Sox (1969)
Position: Manager

Eddie came to the Eastern Shore League with Centreville in 1941, but appeared in fewer than 10 games that year; no statistical data is available on him in the ESL.

He managed the Boston Red Sox for nine games in 1969, etching a 5-4 record. The Bosox had an overall third place finish that year. Pop was also an active major league coach for many years.

*PORTER, Richard Twilley "Twitchy"
Born: 12-30-01, Princess Anne, Md.
Died: 9-24-74, Philadelphia, Penna.
BL   TR   5'10"   170 lbs.
Major Leagues: Cleveland Indians (1929–34), Boston Red Sox (1934)
Position: OF
Career Average: .308

Porter joined the Baltimore Orioles after attending St. John's College in Annapolis. He led the International League in hitting in 1927 with a .376 average. His best season was in 1930 when he hit .350 for the Indians (including 43 doubles) and scored 100 runs. In 1932 he scored 106 runs and hit .308 on the year.

The Eastern Shore native spent six seasons in the major leagues with the Cleveland Indians and a portion of the 1934 season with the Boston Red Sox. He hit over .300 for four of those six years.

Porter managed the Syracuse Chiefs of the International League in the late thirties.

He earned his nickname, "Twitchy Twilley," because of the peculiar manner in which he twirled a bat while stepping into a pitch. Porter was regarded as one of the more colorful players in the game.

POWELL, Raymond Reath "Rabbit"
Born: 11-20-88, Siloam Springs, Ark.
Died: 10-16-62, Chillicothe, Mo.
BL   TR   5'9"   160 lbs.
ESL: Easton, Md. (1939–40)
Major Leagues: Detroit Tigers (1913), Boston Braves (1917–24)
Position: Manager/OF
Career Average: .268

Rabbit played nine years in the major leagues. He led the National League in triples (18) in 1921. He hit .306 that year and hit .302 in 1923. Powell played in 826 games in his major league career (all in the outfield).

QUEEN, Melvin Joseph "Mel"
Born: 3-4-18, Maxwell, Penna.
Died: 4-4-82, Fort Smith, Ark.
BR   TR   6'1/2"   240 lbs.
ESL: Dover, Del. (1938)
Major Leagues: New York Yankees (1942–47), Pittsburgh Pirates (1947–52)
Position: P
Career Record: 27–40

Mel did not see much action for the 1938 Dover club of the ESL, pitching fewer than 45 innings and going 1 for 15 (.067) at bat.

His best year in the majors was 1944, when he was 6–3 for the Yankees, with a 3.31 ERA. He appeared in 39 games for the 1951 Pirates, compiling a 7–9 record.

Queen spent 10 years in the majors with the Yankees and Pirates and his son, Mel, Jr., pitched in the majors in the sixties.

RAFFENSBERGER, Kenneth David
"Ken"
Born: 8-8-17, York, Penna.
Address: 418 Clover Dr., York, Penna.
    17402
BR   TL   6'2"   185 lbs.
ESL: Cambridge, Md. (1937)
Major Leagues:
   St. Louis Cardinals (1939)
   Chicago Cubs (1940–41)
   Philadelphia Phillies (1943–47)
   Cincinnati Reds (1947–54)
Position: P
Career Record: 119–154

Ken holds the Eastern Shore League record for innings pitched (298) in 1937 for the Cambridge Cardinals. He was 18–6 that year with 21 complete games and 183 strikeouts. Raffensberger graduated from the Cambridge Class D ESL club to Rochester in 1938.

He was the winning pitcher in the 1944 all-star game. Ironically, he also led the National League in losses that year with 20, but had a most respectable 3.06 ERA.

Kenny led the league with six saves in 1946. He also led the league with five shutouts in 1949 (19–17). He started 38 games in 1949 (the most in the league), pitching 284 innings. Raffensberger led the league with six shutouts in 1952. He also hit four home runs in his career.

Today Raffensberger is employed with York Capital Distributors in York, Penna.

RAMBERT, Elmer Donald "Pep"
Born: 8-1-17, Cleveland, Ohio
Died: 11-16-74, West Palm Beach, Fla.
BR   TR   6'   175 lbs.
ESL: Federalsburg, Md. (1947)
Major Leagues: Pittsburgh Pirates (1939–40)
Position: 1B/Manager
Career Record: 0–1

Rambert appeared in five major league games for the Pirates as a pitcher, with one start; he pitched a total of 12 innings in the big leagues from 1939 to 1940.

Perhaps "Pep" should have been used at first base instead of as a pitcher in the major leagues. That is what he did with himself as manager of the Federalsburg club in 1947 and the results were quite impressive. He won the Eastern Shore League batting title with a .376 average with 138 hits, 227 total bases, 28 doubles, and 19 home runs.

RENSA, Tony George "Pug"
Born: 9-29-01, Parsons, Penna.
Died: 1-4-87, Wilkes-Barre, Penna.
BR   TR   5'10"   180 lbs.
ESL: Crisfield, Md. (1925)
Major Leagues: Detroit Tigers (1930), Philadelphia Phillies (1930–32), New York
               Yankees (1933), Chicago White Sox (1937–39)
Position: 1B/C
Career Average: .261

Tony played in 85 games for the 1925 Crisfield Crabbers of the Eastern Shore League. He hit .274 that year, with 15 home runs and 146 total bases while playing mostly at first base. He tied the ESL batting average record at .388 in 1926.

His best year at the plate in the major leagues was his rookie year, which was split between the Tigers and the Phillies: He hit .282 on a full-time basis while doing the catching duties.

Rensa caught a total of 185 games in his major league career.

PAUL RICHARDS
MANAGER • BALTIMORE

RICHARDS, Paul Rapier
Born: 11-21-08, Waxahachie, Tex.
Died: 5-4-86, Waxahachie, Tex.
BR   TR   6'1½"   180 lbs.
ESL: Crisfield, Md. (1927)
Major Leagues:
  Brooklyn Dodgers (1932)
  New York Giants (1933–35)
  Philadelphia Athletics (1935)
  Detroit Tigers (1943–46)
Position: C
Career Average: .227

Richards had a great year in the Eastern Shore League in 1927, playing in 87 games and hitting .323 with 107 hits and 198 total bases. He led the ESL in home runs with 24 that year.

His best year at the plate in the major leagues was 1945 with the Tigers, when he hit .256 with 32 RBIs. Richards played in one World Series, going 4 for 19.

He caught 486 games in his major league playing career. He also caught seven games in World Series play. Richards managed for 12 years in the American League. He had the reins of the Chicago White Sox from 1951 to 1954 with three third-place finishes. His 1954 White Sox team won 91 games, but that was still only good enough for a third-place finish.

Richards took over the Baltimore Orioles in 1955 and his best finish was a second place in 1960.

After 15 years' absence from his managing career he was recalled to lead the Chisox in 1976.

His twelve-year overall regular season record as manager was 1,833 games, 929 wins, and 891 losses, for a percent of .510.

*ROBINSON, Warren Grant "Sheriff"
Born: 9-8-21, Cambridge, Md.
Address: 305 Oakley St., Cambridge, Md. 21613
BR   TR   6'1"   195 lbs.
Major Leagues: New York Mets (1964–67)
Position: Coach

Sheriff was signed by Pop Kelchner in 1937 and served as a bull pen catcher for the St. Louis Cardinals. He began his active professional playing career in 1938 as a catcher with Williamson of the Mountain State League and later spent six years in the International League with Rochester and Baltimore.

As a player he led the International League catchers in double plays with 11 in 1942 while with Rochester. He ended his playing career in 1953.

Robinson then began his managing career in Class D leagues and worked his way up to AAA (Richmond) in 1962. He joined the Mets organization the following year. In 1963 while managing at Quincy of the Midwest League he was replaced by former Eastern Shore League manager Walt Millies on August 5.

Sheriff today lives in his hometown of Cambridge and is Dorchester County Treasurer—replacing none other than the late Fred Lucas.

RUFFING, Charles Herbert "Red"
Born: 5-3-04, Granville, Ill.
Died: 2-17-86, Beachwood, Ohio
BR   TR   6'1½"   205 lbs.
ESL: Dover, Del. (1924)
Major Leagues:
  Boston Red Sox (1924–30)
  New York Yankees (1930–46)
  Chicago White Sox (1947)
Position: P
Career Record: 273–225

Ruffing posted a 4–7 record for Dover in 1924 while pitching 94 innings. His .265 batting average gave notice of his value at the plate that 1924 ESL season, as later in the majors he hit .364 in 1930, .330 in 1931, .306 in 1932, and .303 in 1941. He hit 97 doubles (a record for pitchers) and had 273 RBIs (best by a pitcher). His 36 career home runs hold the third best record in history, only two short of Wes Ferrell's 38. His 58 pinch hits rate second on the all-time list for pitchers.

In 1928 Ruffing had 25 complete games for the Red Sox to lead the American League, although the Bosox finished last. On August 13, 1932, he hit a home run in the tenth inning to win his own game over Washington 1–0. On the same date in 1939 he collected four hits and shut out the A's 21–0 in a game called after eight innings.

He twice led the American League with the highest complete game percentage for a pitcher. In 1936 he completed 76 percent (25 of 33) and in 1939 he logged a 79 percent (22 of 28).

Red Ruffing of the New York Yankees won five games by shutout scores of at least 15–0, including defeating the A's 21–0. He also won 18–0, 17–0, and 15–0 twice. Of course when Ruffing pitched, there were nine good hitters in the lineup, since the powerhouse Yankees were supplemented by Ruffing's own powerful bat, which produced 36 homers and a greater output of RBIs than any other modern pitcher. He hit the most exciting grand-slam home run for a pitcher on August 14, 1933, off hurler Weiland of Boston in the bottom of the ninth inning with the score tied 2–2.

Ruffing pitched on seven consecutive New York Yankee pennant-winning teams. He appeared in seven World Series, compiling a 7–2 record.

He compiled season records of 20–7, 21–7, 21–7 in 1937–38–39.

Red Ruffing of the White Sox was the oldest player in 1947 in the major leagues at age 43. He had pitched in the majors for 22 years.

Ruffing was inducted into the Hall of Fame in 1967.

RULLO, Joseph Vincent "Joe"
Born: 6-16-16, New York, N.Y.
Died: 10-28-69, Philadelphia, Penna.
BR   TR   5'11"   168 lbs.
ESL: Federalsburg, Md. (1939)
Major Leagues: Philadelphia Athletics (1943–44)
Position: 2B
Career Average: .212

Joe was one of the great defensive infielders in the ESL and led the league for second basemen in 1939 with a .980 fielding percentage based on 161 putouts and 186 assists, while making only seven errors in 112 games. He also carried a decent bat that year, hitting .245 with 115 hits, 173 total bases, and 91 runs scored.

Rullo appeared in 51 games in the major leagues, hitting .291 his rookie season with the Athletics.

SANFORD, John Stanley "Jack"
BR   TR   6'   190 lbs.
Born: 5-18-29, Wellesley Hills, Mass.
Address: 2300 Presidential Way, West
              Palm Beach, Fla. 33401
ESL: Dover, Del. (1948)
Major Leagues:
  Philadelphia Phillies (1956–58)
  San Francisco Giants (1959–64)
  California Angels (1965–66)
  Kansas City Athletics (1967)
Position: P
Career Record: 137–101

Jack got off to shaky start with the ESL at Dover in 1948, logging a 2–9 mound record with a 7.28 ERA in 18 games.

Sanford toiled for seven years in the minor leagues, winning a total of 83 games before moving up. He was a 19-game winner as a 28-year-old rookie with the Phillies in 1957 and was named National League Rookie of the Year.

He tied the Phillies' single-game strikeout record with 13, against the Cubs on June 7, 1957.

He led the National League in shutouts in 1959 while with the San Francisco Giants with a total of six shutouts. Jack was 24–7 in 1962, including 16 wins in a row with the Giants as they won the National League pennant.

Today he is a Baltimore Oriole scout and golf professional.

SAUER, Edward "Horn"
Born: 1-3-20, Pittsburgh, Penna.
Died: 7-88, Sunland, Calif.
BR   TR   6'1"   188 lbs.
ESL: Easton, Md. (1940)
Major Leagues: Chicago Cubs (1943–45), St. Louis Cardinals (1949), Boston Braves (1949)
Position: OF
Career Average: .256

The brother of famed baseball player Hank Sauer, Ed appeared in 49 games for the Easton club in 1940, hitting .279 on the season.

He appeared in one World Series as a pinch hitter on two occasions without getting a hit.

SELKIRK, George Alexander "Twinkletoes"
Born: 1-4-08, Huntsville, Ont., Canada
Died: 1-19-88, Ft. Lauderdale, Fla.
BL   TR   6'1"   182 lbs.
ESL: Cambridge, Md. (1927)
Major Leagues: New York Yankees (1934–42)
Position: OF
Career Average: .290

Most Eastern Shore League fans knew George wasn't going to be in Class D ball for long when he came to Cambridge in 1927 and in 35 games hit .349, going 39 for 112.

He hit over .300 five times for the Yankees including his first four years in the major leagues. Selkirk showed good power, hitting home runs of 18 ('36), 18 ('37), 21 ('39), and 19 ('40) during the regular season.

George appeared in six World Series with the Yankees, hitting .265 overall in 18 games.

He should be remembered not just as the man who replaced Babe Ruth in right field for the New York Yankees, but for his own accomplishments.

157

*SHOCKLEY, John Costen
Born: 2-8-42, Georgetown, Del.
Address: 405 Walter St., Georgetown, Del. 19947
BL   TL   6'2"   200 lbs.
Major Leagues: Philadelphia Phillies (1964), California Angels (1965)
Position: 1B
Career Average: .197

John broke in with the Philadelphia Phillies in 1964, appearing in 11 games and hitting .229 with one home run. He was 0 for 2 as a pinch hitter.

Shockley was traded to the California Angels in 1965 and got into 40 games, hitting .187 with two home runs and 17 RBIs.

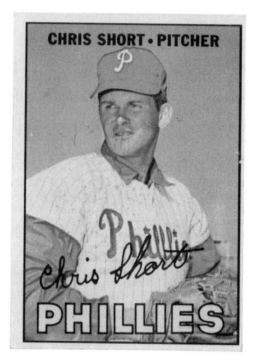

*SHORT, Christopher Joseph "Chris"
Born: 9-19-37, Milford, Del.
Address: 1609 Barnaby St., Newark, Del.
        19702
BR   TL   6'4"   205 lbs.
Major Leagues:
    Philadelphia Phillies (1959–72)
    Milwaukee Brewers (1973)
Position: P
Career Record: 135–132

Chris made his major league debut with the Phillies in 1959. On September 13, 1963, he set a Phillies club record for a left-handed pitcher by striking out 14 in a 3–2 victory over the Dodgers.

Short was the winning pitcher in the final game ever played at the Polo Grounds on September 18, 1963, when the Phillies beat the Mets 5–1. He was 17–9 in 1964, 18–11 in 1965, 20–10 in 1966, and 19–13 in 1968. He struck out 237 batters in 1965.

Short went to the Milwaukee Brewers in his final major league season in 1973 and posted a 3–5 record.

Today he is an insurance agent.

SMOOT, Homer
Born: 3-23-78, Galestown, Md.
Died: 3-25-28, Salisbury, Md.
BL   TR   5′10″   180 lbs.
ESL: Salisbury, Md. (1925)
Major Leagues: St. Louis Cardinals (1902–06), Cincinnati Reds (1906)
Position: OF
Career Average: .290

Homer spent five years in the big leagues with the Cardinals and the Reds. He was a model of consistency with a bat in his hands. He hit .311 as a rookie with the 1902 Cardinals and had 20 stolen bases. Homer came back to snub the sophomore jinx, hitting .296 while also scoring 67 runs.

The first Eastern Shore native to play in the major leagues followed up for the 1904 Redbirds, hitting .281 with 23 stolen bases, 66 RBIs, and 58 runs. He hit .311 in 1905 and scored 73 runs.

Smoot's only off year in the majors was his final season in the bigtime. He played with both the Cardinals and the Reds in 1906 and hit .252 in his final season.

Smoot played all 680 major league games in the outfield. He collected 763 hits in the major leagues, including 102 doubles, 45 triples, and 15 home runs.

Homer played in the ESL at the "young" age of 47 following his major league career.

SOUCHOCK, Stephen "Bud"
Born: 3-3-19, Yatesboro, Penna.
Address: 441 SW 55th Terr., Ft.
        Lauderdale, Fla. 33314
BR   TR   6'2"   203 lbs.
ESL: Easton, Md. (1939)
Major Leagues:
  New York Yankees (1946–48)
  Chicago White Sox (1949)
  Detroit Tigers (1951–55)
Position: OF
Career Average: .255

In 65 games with Easton in 1939 Steve hit .257 but showed power—in those 65 games he had 14 doubles, 9 triples, 8 home runs, and 118 total bases.

He hit a sound .302 for the Yankees in 1946 during his rookie year in the majors. He also hit .302 for the Tigers in 1953. Souchock ended his active major league career with a pinch hit single in his final at bat in 1955.

Today he works for baseball's Central Scouting Bureau.

SUDOL, Edward Lawrence
Born: 9-13-20, Passaic, N.J.
Address: 415 Revilo Blvd., Daytona Beach, Fla. 32014
ESL: Pocomoke City, Cambridge (1940)
Major Leagues: National League (1957–74)
Position: Umpire

Sudol, like Napp, originally came to the Eastern Shore League as a player. He was with both Pocomoke City and Cambridge in 1940.

Sudol umpired behind the plate in the longest day game ever played, on May 31, 1964, in the second game of a doubleheader. The game between San Francisco and

New York at New York lasted 7 hours, 23 minutes and went 23 innings before San Francisco won 8–6.

Unfortunately, he also umpired behind the plate for the longest night game (luckily for Ed it was 10 years later) on September 11, 1974, again in New York. This time the game lasted 7 hours, 4 minutes before St. Louis won 4–3.

SURKONT, Matthew Constantine "Max"
Born: 6-16-22, Central Falls, R.I.
Died: 10-8-86, Largo, Fla.
BR   TR   6'1"   195 lbs.
ESL: Cambridge, Md. (1938)
Major Leagues:
   Chicago White Sox (1949)
   Boston Braves (1950–52)
   Milwaukee Braves (1953)
   Pittsburgh Pirates (1954–56)
   New York Giants (1958)
Position: P
Career Record: 61–76

Max started 21 games for Cambridge in 1938, completing 15 while recording a 9–10 record with a 3.13 ERA. He worked 158 innings, striking out 137 batters.

Surkont was 12–16 and 12–13 for the 1951–52 Braves. He set a major league record in 1953 on May 25 when, with the Braves, he had eight consecutive strikeouts in a game against the Reds. Also in 1953 with Milwaukee he had his best percentage year with an 11–5 record (.688).

He was a good hitter, going 63 for 357 in the big leagues.

Surkont was a tavern owner in Pawtucket, R.I., after his retirement from baseball.

TESTA, Nicholas "Nick"
Born: 6-29-28, New York, N.Y.
Address: 2544 Lurting Ave., Bronx, N.Y. 10469
BR   TR   5'8"   180 lbs.
ESL: Seaford, Del. (1947)
Major Leagues: San Francisco Giants (1958)
Position: C
Career Average: .000

Nick set a record in the 1947 Eastern Shore League but would just as soon forget it—he was charged with 21 passed balls for the Seaford Eagles.

He played in the major leagues in just one game for the Giants in 1958.

Although Testa was once featured by Bill Libby in *The Fireside Book of Baseball* in an article titled "Portrait of a Baseball Failure," he is still one of those guys who just love the game. He keeps active in the sport now by pitching batting practice for both Yankees and Mets occasionally.

Today he is a physical education instructor at Lehman College and his hobby is body building.

THOMPSON, Charles Lemoine "Tim"
Born: 3-1-24, Coalport, Penna.
Address: 536 Summit Dr., Lewistown,
          Penna. 17044
BL   TR   5'11"   190 lbs.
ESL: Cambridge, Md. (1947)
Major Leagues:
    Brooklyn Dodgers (1954)
    Kansas City Athletics (1956–57)
    Detroit Tigers (1958)
Position: C
Career Average: .238

One of the all-time Cambridge Dodger fans' favorite players, Tim hit .349 with 129 RBIs and 219 total bases in 1947 and set an Eastern Shore League record with 14 triples.

He hit .303 for Newport News in 1949 and .296 at St. Paul in 1951.

Tim spent seven years in the minors climaxed by being voted the International League's all-star catcher for the second straight year in 1953.

He batted .303 at Montreal (60 RBIs).

Thompson's best year in the major leagues was 1956 with the Athletics when Tim hit .272 with 13 doubles and 27 RBIs.

Today he is a scouting supervisor for the St. Louis Cardinals.

THOMPSON, Donald Newlin
Born: 12-28-23, Swepsonville, N.C.
Address: 87 E. Euclid Pkwy., Asheville, N.C. 28804
BL   TL   6'   185 lbs.
ESL: Milford, Del. (1947)
Major Leagues: Boston Braves (1949), Brooklyn Dodgers (1951–54)
Position: OF
Career Average: .218

Don hit .242 for the 1953 Dodgers. His batting average of .218 in the major leagues exceeded by one the number of games he played in (217). Thompson managed to make it to a World Series, however, playing in one game and going 0 for 2.

Today he is a realtor for Preferred Properties in Asheville, N.C.

THOMPSON, John Samuel "Jocko"
Born: 1-17-20, Beverly, Mass.
Address: 10 Bel Pre Court, Rockville, Md. 20853
BL   TL   6'   185 lbs.
ESL: Centreville, Md. (1940)
Major Leagues: Philadelphia Phillies (1948–51)
Position: P
Career Record: 6–11

Jocko made a great first impression among ESL fans when he debuted with Centreville in '40 and led the league in strikeouts with 268 and notched 19 wins in the process. He then spent four years in the military earning numerous decorations.

Jocko returned to baseball with Scranton and posted a 15–7 record. He played with Toronto in 1947 and 1948.

Thompson pitched in his first major league game in September 1948, defeating the Cincinnati Reds on a five-hitter. Altogether, he appeared in 41 games in the major leagues. In 1951 (his final year) he was in 29 games and posted a 4–8 record with a 3.85 ERA. He started 14 games that year.

Today he is a government sales coordinator for General Binding Corp.

TOLSON, Chester Julius "Chick"
Born: 11-6-01, Washington, D.C.
Died: 4-16-65, Washington, D.C.
BR   TR   6′   185 lbs.
ESL: Salisbury, Md. (1923)
Major Leagues: Cleveland Indians (1925), Chicago Cubs (1926–30)
Position: 1B
Career Average: .284

Chick had a super year with the Salisbury club both at bat and in the field during the 1923 Eastern Shore League season. In 57 games he hit .355 with 180 total bases, including 14 doubles and 27 home runs. At first base he led the league with a .995 fielding average while handling 570 putouts and 19 assists with just three errors.

   Chick played in one World Series, going hitless in a pinch hit appearance. He hit .313 for the Cubs in 1926, .296 in 1927, and .300 in his final 1930 season. He led the National League in pinch hitting in 1926, going 14 for 40.

TRECHOK, Frank Adam
Born: 12-24-15, Windber, Penna.
Address: 4600 29th Ave. S., Minneapolis, Minn. 55406
BR   TR   5′10″   175 lbs.
ESL: Salisbury, Md. (1937)
Major Leagues: Washington Senators (1937)
Position: SS
Career Average: .500

Frank had a super year for a super Salisbury team in 1937 as he appeared in 96 games, hitting .338 for the pennant champions. He also scored 93 runs, had 20 doubles, 19 home runs, and 84 RBIs as a result of his 131 hits. He also led the ESL in total bases with 210. No wonder he was called up by the Senators when Salisbury completed their regular season.

   Frank didn't stay in the major leagues long, however, as he appeared in one game that 1937 season and went 2 for 4. Not many can say they hit .500 for a major league career.

VALO, Elmer William
Born: 3-5-21, Ribnik, Czechoslovakia
Address: 571 Columbia Ave., Palmerton,
Penna. 18071
BL   TR   5'11"   190 lbs.
ESL: Federalsburg, Md. (1939)
Major Leagues:
  Philadelphia Phillies (1940–54)
  Kansas City Athletics (1955–56)
  Philadelphia Phillies (1956)
  Brooklyn Dodgers (1957)
  Los Angeles Dodgers (1958)
  Cleveland Indians (1959)
  New York Yankees (1960)
  Washington Senators (1960)
  Minnesota Twins (1961)
  Philadelphia Phillies (1961)
Position: OF
Career Average: .282

Valo appeared in 34 games for Federalsburg in 1939, hitting .374 while in the ESL. Little did anyone know in 1939, though, that young Elmer Valo would one day join Micky Vernon in being the only two former Eastern Shore League players to be employed in the major leagues from the thirties into the sixties—only Valo never got credit for it.

Here is the story of how he became one of the select few to play in four decades in the major leagues, even though official records do not reveal this fact. Valo was called up to the Philadelphia Athletics late in the 1939 season; he appeared as a pinch hitter and walked in his only time at bat on the final day of the '39 season. The scorekeeper (a young sportswriter named Red Smith) told A's manager Connie Mack that Valo had not been officially signed to a contract and so Valo's name was never entered into the scorebook. But what did go in the scorebook?

In 1949 he hit two bases-loaded triples. He is the only player to ever play on two different major league teams that lost 20 or more consecutive games: the '43 A's, who lost 20 straight, and the '61 Phillies, who lost 23 in a row. He moved in franchise shifts on three occasions: with the A's from Philadelphia to Kansas City; with the Dodgers from Brooklyn to Los Angeles; and from the Washington Senators to the Minnesota Twins.

Valo had 90 career pinch hits and hit over .300 five times. His best year was with the 1955 Kansas City A's, when he hit .364 and was 14 for 31 as a pinch hitter. His was a long and outstanding professional baseball career.

Valo was unofficially in the majors 23 years, officially for 22. He was also known for risking injury while running into walls to make catches.

Today Valo is a full-time scout for the Phillies and is loaded with baseball stories.

CHRIS VAN CUYK

VAN CUYK, Christian Gerald "Chris"
Born: 3-1-27, Kimberly, Wisc.
Address: 14405 Amy Lane, Hudson, Fla.
    33562
BL   TL   6'6"   215 lbs.
ESL: Cambridge, Md. (1946–47)
Major Leagues:
    Brooklyn Dodgers (1950–52)
Position: P
Career Record: 7–11

A big 6'6" lefty, Van Cuyk was the mound terror of the 1947 Eastern Shore League. He posted a 25–2 record, with 24 complete games, nine shutouts, and 247 strikeouts—all league-leading statistics and the nine shutouts a league record. His .926 winning percentage of 1947 is fifth all-time best in minor league history.

He was 11–4 at Montreal and later toiled for Fort Worth, winning 14 games before being promoted to Brooklyn. Chris appeared in 44 games for the Dodgers and had 66 strikeouts in 97 innings in 1952.

He is now retired from the Portland Cement Company.

166

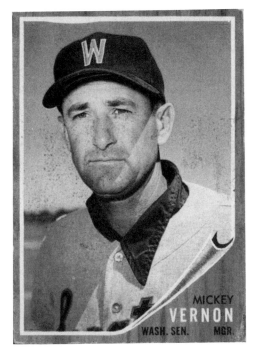

VERNON, James Barton "Mickey"
Born: 4-22-18, Marcus Hook, Penna.
Address: 100 E. Rose Valley Rd.,
　　　　　Wallingford, Penna. 19086
BL　TL　6'2"　170 lbs.
ESL: Easton, Md. (1937)
Major Leagues:
　Washington Senators (1939–48)
　Cleveland Indians (1949)
　Washington Senators (1950–55)
　Boston Red Sox (1956–57)
　Cleveland Indians (1958)
　Milwaukee Braves (1959)
　Pittsburgh Pirates (1960)
Position: 1B
Career Average: .286

Vernon played 83 games for Easton in 1937, hitting .287 with 24 doubles, 10 home runs, and 64 RBIs.

One of the greatest and most durable of all the ESL graduates, he played in four decades and joined Elmer Valo from the ESL in that distinction.

Vernon (not Lou Gehrig) holds the major league record for most games played by a first baseman. He played 2,237 games at first base. He hit over .300 four times, won two American League batting titles (.353 in 1946 and .337 in 1953), and led the American League in doubles in '53 (43) and '54 (33).

Vernon was manager of Washington Senators from 1961 to 1963.

VOYLES, Philip Vance
Born: 5-12-00, Murphy, N.C.
Died: 11-3-72, Marlboro, Mass.
BL　TR　5'11½"　175 lbs.
ESL: Parksley, Va. (1925)
Major Leagues: Boston Braves (1929)
Position: OF
Career Average: .235

Voyles led the ESL in total hits (119) in 1925 while he was with Parksley, and had a batting average of .350 on the season. He also had 11 home runs and 17 doubles.

Phil went to Columbia, Haverhill, Williamsport, Baltimore, Newark, Harrisburg, and Jeannette before making it to Boston in 1929. He appeared in 20 major league games as an outfielder for the Braves, going 16 for 68.

Voyles played with seven minor league teams in 1930 before being released in 1931. He attempted a brief comeback in 1934, but was unsuccessful.

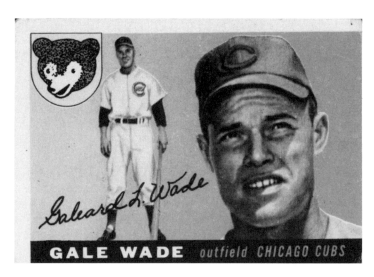

GALE WADE outfield CHICAGO CUBS

WADE, Galeard Lee "Gale"
Born: 1-20-29, Hollister, Mo.
Address: RR 1, Nebo, N.C. 28761
BL   TR   6'1½"   185 lbs.
ESL: Cambridge, Md. (1948)
Major Leagues:
  Chicago Cubs (1955–56)
Position: OF
Career Average: .133

Wade led each league he played in for stolen bases for four straight seasons, including 55 steals at Elmira in 1952. He moved up to the minor league system at Indianapolis in '54. Gale was originally signed as a pitcher, but an injured arm moved him to outfield. He went 6 for 33 his rookie season in 1955 with one double and one home run.

Wade is now an electrician in Nebo, N.C.

WALLAESA, John "Jack"
Born: 8-31-19, Easton, Penna.
Died: 12-27-86, Easton, Penna.
BR   TR   6'3"   191 lbs.
ESL: Federalsburg, Md. (1939)
Major Leagues: Philadelphia Athletics (1940–46), Chicago White Sox (1947–48)
Position: SS
Career Average: .205

Jack was a slick fielding shortstop for the ESL Federalsburg A's in 1939 and led the league in fielding for shortstops with a .961 percentage, making only seven errors. He played in 40 games with a .206 batting average.

Wallaesa hit .256 for the 1942 Athletics in the major leagues. While with the White

Sox in 1948 he decided to try and further his career by learning to switch-hit and batted .188 his final year in the majors.

WEST, Richard Thomas "Dick"
Born: 11-24-15, Louisville, Ky.
Address: P.O. Box 5095, Fort Wayne, Ind. 46805
BR   TR   6'2"   180 lbs.
ESL: Dover, Del. (1938)
Major Leagues: Cincinnati Reds (1938–43)
Position: C
Career Average: .221

Dick had played in just 43 games with the Dover club in the ESL when he was called up to the major leagues. But consider what he did in those 43 games: He hit .434, 12 doubles, 22 home runs, 61 RBIs, 161 total bases, and 18 stolen bases. The only trouble was, however, he never quite duplicated such stats in the majors.

He did manage a .393 average on a part-time basis in 1940, and had a full season with the Reds in 1941, but hit only .215 on the season.

WILHELM, Charles Ernest "Spider"
Born: 5-23-29, Baltimore, Md.
Address: 1490 Sanderling Dr., Englewood, Fla. 33533
BR   TR   5'9"   170 lbs.
ESL: Federalsburg, Md. (1947)
Major Leagues: Philadelphia Athletics (1953)
Position: SS
Career Average: .286

Wilhelm set the Eastern Shore League record for most at bats in one season in 1947, when he came to the plate 518 times.

Spider played in seven games for the Philadelphia A's in 1953, going 2 for 7. He went 1 for 1 as a pinch hitter.

Today he is a retired fire prevention bureau inspector in Baltimore.

WITTIG, John Carl "Johnnie"
Born: 6-16-14, Baltimore, Md.
Address: 163 Stafford St., Baltimore, Md. 21227
BR   TR   6'   180 lbs.
ESL: Dover, Del. (1937)
Major Leagues: New York Giants (1938–43), Boston Red Sox (1949)
Position: P
Career Record: 10–25

Wittig was a real hummer with his fastball in the ESL, but had a little trouble with his control. He hurled 198 innings that year and recorded 196 strikeouts while completing 13 games. He posted an 8–12 record for Dover. He also led the ESL in walks issued that year with 112.

John appeared in 40 games for the Giants in 1943 but went 5–15 with a 4.23 ERA. He was 2–2 as a relief pitcher with four saves.

YARYAN, Clarence Everett "Yam"
Born: 11-5-93, Knowlton, Iowa
Died: 11-16-64, Birmingham, Ala.
BR   TR   5'10"   180 lbs.
ESL: Easton, Md. (1939)
Major Leagues: Chicago White Sox (1921–22)
Position: C
Career Average: .260

Yam spent 19 years in the minor leagues and posted a career minor league batting average of .316 for his efforts.

He came to Easton of the ESL in 1939 and in 22 games hit .229 with 16 hits.

YERKES, Charles Carroll "Lefty"
Born: 6-13-03, Mc Sherrystown, Penna.
Died: 12-20-50, Oakland, Calif.
BR   TL   5'11"   162 lbs.
ESL: Dover, Del. (1926)
Major Leagues: Philadelphia Athletics (1927–29), Chicago Cubs (1932–33)
Position: P
Career Record: 1–1

Lefty posted an 18–7 won-lost record for Dover in 1926, working 203 innings and striking out 110 batters.

He appeared in 19 games for the Athletics in 1929, posting a 1–0 record. He started two games that year and worked in 37 innings, his most productive season in the majors.

YOUSE, Walter
ESL: Seaford, Del. (1946)
Major Leagues: Currently Scouting Supervisor of Milwaukee Brewers
Position: Manager

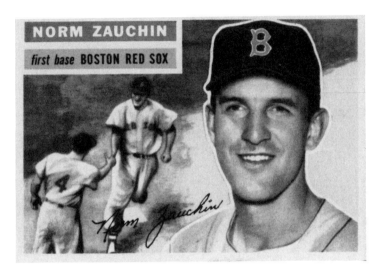

ZAUCHIN, Norbert Henry "Norm"
Born: 11-17-29, Royal Oak, Mich.
Address: 818 N. Montez Dr., Thomas
    Acres, Ala. 35020
BR   TR   6'4½"   220 lbs.
ESL: Milford, Del. (1948)
Major Leagues:
  Boston Red Sox (1951–57)
  Washington Senators (1958–59)
Position: 1B
Career Average: .233

Zauchin put on the greatest one-man batting display in the history of the Eastern Shore League in 1948 and set four ESL batting records in the process. With the Milford Red Sox that year in 120 games he scored 126 runs, had 170 hits, 324 total bases, 44 doubles, 33 home runs, 138 RBIs, and a .353 batting average. The doubles, home runs, RBIs, and total bases are ESL standards.

The following year he went to San Jose and then belted 35 homers for Birmingham in 1950. At Louisville in 1951 he had 104 RBIs. He hit his career high 42 home runs in 1953.

In 1954 at Louisville he led the American Association in RBIs and he was also top defensive first baseman in the league. In 1955 for the Boston Red Sox Zauchin had 27 home runs and 93 RBIs. In a game against the Washington Senators on May 27, 1955, he hit three home runs and had 10 RBIs.

Today Zauchin is an account executive for Hart Hanks Company in Thomas Acres, Ala.

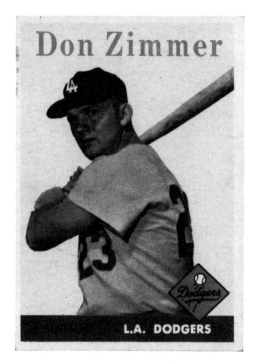

Don Zimmer

L.A. DODGERS

ZIMMER, Donald William "Don"
Born: 1-17-31, Cincinnati, Ohio
Address: 10124 Yacht Club Dr., St.
          Petersburg, Fla. 33706
BR   TR   5'9"   165 lbs.
ESL: Cambridge, Md. (1949)
Major Leagues:
  Brooklyn Dodgers (1954–57)
  Los Angeles Dodgers (1958–59)
  Chicago Cubs (1960–61)
  New York Mets (1962)
  Cincinnati Reds (1962)
  Los Angeles Dodgers (1963)
  Washington Senators (1963–65)
Position: SS
Career Average: .235

Zimmer played in 71 games with the 1949 Cambridge club, hitting .227 with 101 total bases, including 14 doubles and 26 stolen bases.

He led the PONY League in home runs and stolen bases in 1950, and in 1952 at Mobile he batted .310. Zimmer followed with a .300 season at St. Paul in 1953 before being hit on the head with a pitch. Zimmer received two brain operations as a result of the incident. Until then, he had been moving right on schedule with the Dodger organization. He was listed in critical condition for several weeks and was unconscious for two weeks.

Zim was married at home plate in 1951 while with the Eastern League.

Zimmer played on the 1955 and 1959 Dodger championship teams.

This gutty guy wouldn't stay away from the great game even after another nasty beaning in 1956 when he was hit in the face and suffered eye damage.

Zimmer hit .262 for the 1958 Dodgers with 15 doubles, 17 home runs, and 60 RBIs. Today he is the manager of the Chicago Cubs.

Eastern Shore League Statistics

EASTERN SHORE LEAGUE PENNANT WINNERS

1922	Parksley, Va.	(.627)	
1923	Dover, Del.	(.680)	
1924	Parksley, Va.	(.575)	
1925	Cambridge, Md.	(.573)	
1926	Crisfield, Md.	(.750)	
1927	Parksley, Va.	(.653)	
1937	Salisbury, Md.	(.615)	Jake Flowers, Manager
1938	Salisbury, Md.	(.580)	Jake Flowers
1939	Federalsburg, Md.	(.686)	Sam Holbrook
1940	Dover, Del.	(.600)	John Clark
1941	Milford, Del.	(.611)	Hal Gruber
1946	Centreville, Md.	(.704)	Jim McLeod
1947	Cambridge, Md.	(.728)	Roy Nichols
1948	Salisbury, Md.	(.736)	Gene Corbett
1949	Easton, Md.	(.567)	Jack Farmer

EASTERN SHORE LEAGUE PLAY-OFF WINNERS
(If different from pennant champion)

The top four teams in the regular season standings played a round-robin series to determine the play-off champion. For example, in 1949 Federalsburg finished first (4–1), Rehoboth Beach second (4–2), Easton third (2–4), and Salisbury fourth (1–4). Rehoboth Beach then defeated Federalsburg in the finals, four games to three.

1939	Cambridge, Md.	Fred Lucas, Manager
1940	Salisbury, Md.	Gus Brittain & Ed Kobesky
1941	Easton, Md.	Dal Warren
1947	Seaford, Del.	Bobby Westfall
1948	Milford, Del.	Clayton Sheedy
1949	Rehoboth Beach, Del.	Bill Sisler

EASTERN SHORE LEAGUE BATTING RECORDS

CATEGORY	PLAYER	TEAM	YEAR	RECORD
Average	Don Maxa	Easton	1948	.382*
Hits	Ray Jablonski	Milford	1948	172
Runs scored	Jimmy Stevens	Centreville	1946	132
Doubles	Norm Zauchin	Milford	1948	44
Triples	Tim Thompson	Cambridge	1947	14
Home runs	Norm Zauchin	Milford	1948	33
RBIs	Norm Zauchin	Milford	1948	138
Total bases	Norm Zauchin	Milford	1948	323
At bats	Charles Wilhelm	Federalsburg	1947	518
Stolen bases	Don Nicholas	Cambridge	1948	82
Strikeouts	Hal Harrigan	Milford	1939	137
Walks	Bobby Tripp	Dover	1947	133
Sacrifices	Whitey Koppenhaver	Salisbury	1948	22
Hit by pitcher	Pete Kousagan	Easton	1946	19

*Tony Rensa of Crisfield and McDonald of Dover hit .388 in 1925 and 1923 respectively but league statisticians never credited them with the batting average record, probably because most records date back only to the 1937 season. The batting average marks mentioned are the only records that pre-date any set from 1937 forward.

EASTERN SHORE LEAGUE PITCHING RECORDS

CATEGORY	PLAYER	TEAM	YEAR	RECORD
Winning percent	Joe Kohlman	Salisbury	1937	.962* (25–1)
Total wins	Les Hinckle	Federalsburg	1939	27
Complete games	Les Hinckle	Federalsburg	1939	29
	John Andre	Seaford	1948	29
Strikeouts	Les Hinckle	Federalsburg	1939	309
Innings pitched	Ken Raffensberger	Cambridge	1937	298
Shutouts	Chris Van Cuyk	Cambridge	1947	9
Losses	Newell Valentine	Pocomoke City	1939	17
	Howard Smith	Cambridge	1940	17
Wild pitches	Bill Fogg	Dover	1947	21
Hit batsmen	Steve Colosky	Cambridge	1940	20
Walks	A. Schultz	Salisbury	1949	165
Hits allowed	Lew Krausse	Federalsburg	1946	272
	John Andre	Seaford	1948	272

*All-time minor league record (25 credit games)

EASTERN SHORE LEAGUE PITCHING LEADERS (BY YEAR)

MOST WINS

YEAR	PITCHER	TEAM	TOTAL
1922	Klingehoffer	Parksley	15–5
1923	Sheritzer	Cambridge	13–7
1924	Brown	Parksley	17–8
1925	Firth	Parksley	21–10
1926	Firth	Parksley	21–8
1927	Rose	Crisfield	17–13
1937	Joe Kohlman	Salisbury	25–1
1938	Joe Davis	Cambridge	17–5
	John Bassler	Salisbury	17–5
1939	Les Hinckle	Federalsburg	27–6
1940	Jorge Comellas	Salisbury	21–10

EASTERN SHORE LEAGUE PITCHING LEADERS (BY YEAR) (Cont'd)

MOST WINS (Cont'd)

YEAR	PITCHER	TEAM	TOTAL
1941	Bill Boland	Milford	20–5
1946	Waldt	Centreville	17–7
1947	Chris Van Cuyk	Cambridge	25–2
1948	John Andre	Seaford	21–12
1949	Pinelli	Rehoboth Beach	18–11

COMPLETE GAMES

YEAR	PITCHER	TEAM	TOTAL
1937	Joe Kohlman	Salisbury	23
1938	Joe Davis	Cambridge	21
1939	Les Hinckle	Federalsburg	29
1940	Steve Colosky	Cambridge	21
1946	Mike Gast	Centreville	21
	Lew Krausse	Federalsburg	21
1947	Duke Makowsky	Seaford	24
	Chris Van Cuyk	Cambridge	24
1948	John Andre	Seaford	29
1949	Pinelli	Rehoboth Beach	27

STRIKEOUTS

1922	Klingehoffer	Parksley	158
1923	Firth	Parksley	133
1924	Hearne	Salisbury	175
1925	Firth	Parksley	131
1926	Firth	Parksley	143
1927	Toner	Salisbury	132
1937	Joe Kohlman	Salisbury	257
1938	Bill Yarewick	Milford	207
1939	Les Hinckle	Federalsburg	309
1940	John Thompson	Centreville	268
1941	Chris Hayden	Milford	188

STRIKEOUTS (Cont'd)

YEAR	PITCHER	TEAM	TOTAL
1946	Mike Gast	Centreville	182
1947	Chris Van Cuyk	Cambridge	247
1948	John Andre	Seaford	228
1949	John Andre	Rehoboth Beach	240

INNINGS PITCHED

1922	Schroll	Cambridge	205
1923	R. Perry	Cambridge	187
1924	Hummer	Parksley	221
1925	Miller	Parksley	232
1926	Firth	Parksley	246
1927	Rose	Crisfield	237
1937	Ken Raffensberger	Cambridge	298
1938	Wes Ratteree	Federalsburg	219
1939	Les Hinckle	Federalsburg	283
1940	Jorge Comellas	Salisbury	258
1941	Rudy Rundus	Cambridge	230
1946	Lew Krausse	Federalsburg	216
1947	Duke Makowsky	Seaford	249
1948	John Andre	Seaford	263
1949	Pinelli	Rehoboth Beach	252

BASES ON BALLS

1922	Schroll	Cambridge	76
1923	Hearne	Salisbury	111
1924	Chacomas	Easton	90
1925	Miller	Parksley	116
1926	Skeleton	Salisbury	116
1927	Arthur	Northampton	88
1937	John Wittig	Dover	112
1938	Wayne Lomas	Dover	124

EASTERN SHORE LEAGUE PITCHING LEADERS (BY YEAR) (Cont'd)

BASES ON BALLS (Cont'd)

YEAR	PITCHER	TEAM	TOTAL
1939	Harold Brosman	Centreville	129
1940	John Mikan	Salisbury	136
1941	Tom Leahy	Centreville	99
1946	Walter Doherty	Dover	140
1947	Bob Pirelli	Easton	142
1948	John Andre	Seaford	148
1949	A. Scultz	Salisbury	165

WILD PITCHES

YEAR	PITCHER	TEAM	TOTAL
1922	Klingehoffer	Parksley	9
1923	Zellers	Parksley	14
1924	Perry	Cambridge	9
1925	McKnelly	Easton	6
1938	Wayne Lomas	Centreville	20
1939	Conklyn Merriweather	Easton	18
1940	Charles Norton	Centreville	18
1941	Walter Okypch	Milford	13
1946	John Coakley	Federalsburg	16
1947	Bill Fogg	Dover	21
1948	John Andre	Seaford	14
1949	Henkel	Salisbury	18

HIT BATSMEN

YEAR	PITCHER	TEAM	TOTAL
1938	Wayne Lomas	Centreville	18
1939	Harold Brosman	Centreville	17
1940	Steve Colosky	Cambridge	20
1941	Leo Summers	Cambridge	11
1946	Walter Doherty	Dover	13
	Bill McGurk	Dover	13
1947	Mike Quill	Cambridge	13

HIT BATSMEN (Cont'd)

YEAR	PITCHER	TEAM	TOTAL
	Carroll Mattson	Dover	13
1948	John Andre	Seaford	18
1949	McPhail	Seaford	11

LOSSES

YEAR	PITCHER	TEAM	TOTAL
1922	Goetzel	Parksley	10
1923	R. Perry	Cambridge	11
	Godfrey	Parksley	11
1924	Chacomas	Easton	14
	Miller	Parksley	14
1925	Miller	Parksley	14
1926	Everham	Crisfield	15
1927	Rose	Crisfield	13
1937	Bill Barnes	Crisfield	16
	Nick Finta	Dover	16
1938	Wayne Lomas	Centreville	15
	Bill Boyce	Milford	15
1939	Newell Valentine	Pocomoke City	17
1940	Howard Smith	Cambridge	17
1941	Rudy Rundus	Cambridge	13
	Leo Venskus	Salisbury	13
	Ray McGlaughlin	Federalsburg	13
1946	Charles Storch	Federalsburg	14
	Dean Crooks	Seaford	14
1947	Reed Loveness	Rehoboth Beach	15
1948	George McPhail	Seaford	14
1949	Stu Miller	Salisbury	13

EASTERN SHORE LEAGUE PITCHING LEADERS (BY YEAR) (Cont'd)

HITS ALLOWED

YEAR	PITCHER	TEAM	TOTAL RECORD
1922	Schroll	Cambridge	159
1923	Sheritzer	Cambridge	160
1924	Hummer	Parksley	200
1925	Miller	Parksley	225
1926	Firth	Parksley	229
1927	Rose	Crisfield	258
1937	Frank Radler	Easton	238
1938	Frank Radler	Easton	252
1939	Art Renkowitz	Cambridge	236
1940	Jorge Comellas	Salisbury	252
1941	Leo Venskus	Salisbury	199
1946	Lew Krausse	Federalsburg	272
1947	Lew DeFeo	Federalsburg	252
1948	John Andre	Seaford	272
1949	Pinelli	Rehoboth Beach	252

WINNING PERCENT

YEAR	PITCHER	TEAM	PERCENTAGE
1922	Klingehoffer	Parksley	.750 (15–5)
1923	Humphreys	Dover	.800 (12–3)
1924	Glass	Cambridge	.700 (14–6)
1925	Trippe	Cambridge	.783 (18–5)
1926	Firth	Parksley	.724 (21–8)
1927	Brown	Parksley	.800 (16–4)
1937	Joe Kohlman	Salisbury	.986 (25–1)
1938	Joe Davis	Cambridge	.773 (17–5)
	Bassler	Salisbury	.773 (17–5)
1939	Les Hinckle	Federalsburg	.818 (27–6)
1940	Guy Johnson	Dover	.846 (11–2)
1941	Boland	Milford	.800 (20–5)
1946	Mike Gast	Centreville	.762 (16–5)

WINNING PERCENT (Cont'd)

YEAR	PITCHER	TEAM	PERCENTAGE
1947	Chris Van Cuyk	Cambridge	.926 (25–2)
1948	Herb Moford	Salisbury	.833 (20–4)
1949	Duke Markell	Seaford	.909 (10–1)

EASTERN SHORE LEAGUE BATTING LEADERS (BY YEAR)

AVERAGE

YEAR	PLAYER	TEAM	AVERAGE
1922	Tagg	Crisfield	.329
1923	McDonald	Dover	.388
1924	Mattis	Parksley	.322
1925	St. Martin	Parksley	.363
1926	Rensa	Crisfield	.388
1927	Bickham	Parksley	.361
1937	Jerry Lynn	Salisbury	.342
1938	Sid Gordon	Milford	.352
1939	Martin Steinman	Milford	.378
1940	Lloyd Rice	Federalsburg	.363
1941	Gordon McKinnon	Milford	.344
1946	Sid Langston	Salisbury	.353
1947	Elmer Rambert	Federalsburg	.376
1948	Don Maxa	Easton	.382
1949	Gordon Bragg	Easton	.362

HOME RUNS

YEAR	PLAYER	TEAM	NUMBER
1922	Jake Flowers	Cambridge	14
1923	Tolson	Salisbury	27
1924	Zanzallari	Crisfield	24
1925	St. Martin	Parksley	25
	Fitzberger	Salisbury	25
1926	Stack	Parksley	22
1927	Richards	Crisfield	24

EASTERN SHORE LEAGUE BATTING LEADERS (BY YEAR) (Cont'd)

HOME RUNS (Cont'd)

YEAR	PLAYER	TEAM	NUMBER
1937	Alex Pitko	Centreville	20
1938	Bill Phillips	Federalsburg	31
1939	Henry Schulter	Pocomoke City	29
1940	Ed Kobesky	Salisbury	18
1941	Tommy Koval	Cambridge	16
1946	Don Marshall	Dover	29
1947	Ducky Detweiler	Federalsburg	29
1948	Norm Zauchin	Milford	33
1949	Bob Westfall	Federalsburg	19

TRIPLES

YEAR	PLAYER	TEAM	NUMBER
1922	Hearn	Salisbury	6
1923	Sullivan	Dover	7
1924	Siegle	Cambridge	5
	Johnson	Cambridge	5
1925	Clancy	Dover	15
1926	Sullivan	Dover	13
1927	Nalbach	Northampton	7
	Duggan	Northampton	7
1937	Alex Pitko	Centreville	8
1938	Sid Gordon	Milford	9
1939	Francis Walsh	Centreville	12
1940	Al Mocek	Centreville	6
	Hal Harrigan	Milford	6
	Gordon McKinnon	Milford	6
1941	Tommy Koval	Cambridge	9
1946	Fred Pacitto	Centreville	13
	Bunky Langgood	Centreville	13
1947	Tim Thompson	Cambridge	14
1948	Charley Price	Milford	12
	Tommy Tanner	Rehoboth Beach	12
1949	Ron Berger	Salisbury	11

DOUBLES

YEAR	PLAYER	TEAM	NUMBER
1922	Fisher	Parksley	19
1923	Kraemer	Parksley	17
	Sullivan	Dover	17
1924	Sullivan	Dover	24
1925	Johnson	Cambridge	20
1926	Cather	Easton	31
1927	Lyons	Crisfield	26
1937	Nat Riggin	Crisfield	27
	Harry Boyce	Federalsburg	27
1938	Milton Vergani	Easton	39
1939	Martin Steinman	Milford	39
1940	Norman Jaeger	Milford	37
1941	Gordon McKinnon	Milford	25
1946	Don Ford	Seaford	34
1947	Roy Nichols	Cambridge	35
1948	Norm Zauchin	Milford	44
1949	Bob Westfall	Federalsburg	35

HITS

YEAR	PLAYER	TEAM	NUMBER
1922	Fisher	Parksley	83
1923	McDonald	Dover	95
1924	Sullivan	Dover	97
1925	Voyles	Salisbury	119
1926	McDougall	Parksley	113
	Aikens	Cambridge	113
1927	Bickham	Parksley	119
1937	Bill Luzansky	Salisbury	128
1938	Sid Gordon	Milford	145
1939	Francis Walsh	Centreville	163
1940	Bobby Maier	Salisbury	146
1941	Art Flesland	Milford	157
1946	Fred Pacitto	Centreville	164

EASTERN SHORE LEAGUE BATTING LEADERS (BY YEAR) (Cont'd)

HITS (Cont'd)

YEAR	PLAYER	TEAM	NUMBER
1947	Tim Thompson	Cambridge	162
	Bob Stramm	Cambridge	162
1948	Ray Jablonski	Milford	172
1949	Bob Westfall	Federalsburg	158

RUNS

YEAR	PLAYER	TEAM	NUMBER
1922	Jake Flowers	Cambridge	50
1923	McDonald	Dover	60
1924	Fitzberger	Salisbury	58
1925	St. Martin	Parksley	78
1926	Hohman	Easton	69
1927	McAllister	Parksley	71
1937	Alex Pitko	Centreville	103
1938	George Reisinger	Dover	110
1939	Irving Kolberg	Federalsburg	111
1940	Paul Gaulin	Dover	102
1941	Gordon McKinnon	Milford	98
1946	Jimmy Stevens	Centreville	132
1947	Bob Stramm	Cambridge	129
1948	Norm Zauchin	Milford	126
1949	Bob Westfall	Federalsburg	126

RUNS BATTED IN

YEAR	PLAYER	TEAM	NUMBER
1937	Harvey "Zip" Legates	Federalsburg	81
1938	Jimmy Conlan	Salisbury	127
1939	Francis Walsh	Centreville	129
1940	Fred Lutz	Easton	81
1941	Art Gunning	Milford	67
1946	Don Marshall	Dover	110
1947	Ducky Detweiler	Federalsburg	133
1948	Norm Zauchin	Milford	138
1949	Bob Westfall	Federalsburg	113

TOTAL BASES

YEAR	PLAYER	TEAM	NUMBER
1922	Harnsberger	Pocomoke City	225
1923	Chick Tolson	Salisbury	180
1924	Zanzallari	Crisfield	185
1925	St. Martin	Parksley	215
1926	McDougall	Parksley	179
1927	Paul Richards	Crisfield	198
1937	Frank Trechock	Salisbury	210
1938	Sid Gordon	Milford	256
1939	Francis Walsh	Centreville	292
1940	Vic Weiss	Pocomoke City	226
1941	Tommy Koval	Cambridge	201
1946	Don Marshall	Dover	280
1947	Ducky Detweiler	Federalsburg	269
1948	Norm Zauchin	Milford	323
1949	Bob Westfall	Federalsburg	260

SACRIFICES

YEAR	PLAYER	TEAM	NUMBER
1938	Danny Murtaugh	Cambridge	13
1939	Charles Fitzgerald	Salisbury	21
1940	Ray Murray	Pocomoke City	20
1941	Alvin Kaiser	Cambridge	11
	Bill Morrison	Cambridge	11
1946	Bill Donica	Easton	13
1947	Fred Shipman	Seaford	21
1948	Whitey Koppenhaver	Salisbury	22
1949	Richard Yata	Easton	12

BASES ON BALLS

YEAR	PLAYER	TEAM	NUMBER
1922	Harnsberger	Pocomoke City	43
1924	Earley	Salisbury	44
1925	Eggert	Dover	52
1926	Baker	Crisfield	54

EASTERN SHORE LEAGUE BATTING LEADERS (BY YEAR) (Cont'd)

BASES ON BALLS (Cont'd)

YEAR	PLAYER	TEAM	NUMBER
1927	McAllister	Parksley	55
1938	Ed Leip	Salisbury	92
1939	Bob Jones	Cambridge	72
1940	Charles Vartanian	Salisbury	85
1941	Tommy Koval	Cambridge	74
1946	Mike Colina	Easton	99
1947	Bobby Tripp	Dover	133
1948	Don Nicholas	Cambridge	130
1949	Bill Wilsman	Rehoboth Beach	119

STRUCK OUT

1922	Dittmar	Crisfield	57
1924	Zanzallari	Crisfield	62
1925	Melvin	Easton	74
1926	Hohman	Easton	49
1927	McAllister	Parksley	60
1938	Norward Wurst	Centreville	108
1939	Hal Harrigan	Milford	137
1940	Art Duff	Cambridge	133
1941	Edward Patrow	Cambridge	88
1946	Pete Kousagan	Easton	96
1947	Walter Derucki	Dover	112
1948	Mike Ryan	Easton	112
1949	Bill Flanagan	Salisbury	129

HIT BY PITCHER

1922	McKnight	Pocomoke City	37
1924	Ryan	Cambridge	8
	Lyston	Salisbury	8

HIT BY PITCHER (Cont'd)

YEAR	PLAYER	TEAM	NUMBER
1938	Irving Kolberg	Federalsburg	12
1939	Irving Kolberg	Federalsburg	10
1940	Bob Morem	Salisbury	10
1941	Charles Ziober	Easton	10
1946	Pete Kousagan	Easton	19
1947	Don Petchow	Cambridge	12
	Charles Havelka	Federalsburg	12
1948	Tommy Tanner	Rehoboth Beach	10
1949	John Burnham	Federalsburg	8
	Ralph Betcher	Rehoboth Beach	8

Eastern Shore League 1946–49 Stadium Seating Capacity

PARK	TEAM	CAPACITY
Memorial Field	Salisbury Cardinals	2,800
Dodger Park	Cambridge Dodgers	2,267
Rehoboth Beach Ball Park	Rehoboth Beach Pirates	2,100
Milford Baseball Park	Milford Red Sox	2,000
Dover Ball Park	Dover Phillies	1,800
Federal Park	Federalsburg Athletics	1,800
Federal Park	Easton Yankees	1,500
Seaford Ball Park	Seaford Eagles	1,000

Eastern Shore League Presidents

1922 W. B. Miller (Salisbury)

1923 M. B. Thawley (Crisfield)

1924 J. Harry Rew (Salisbury)

1925 J. Harry Rew (Salisbury)

1926 J. Harry Rew (Salisbury)

1937 J. Thomas Kibler (Chestertown)

1938 Harry S. Russell (Easton)

1939 Harry S. Russell (Easton)

1940 Harry S. Russell (Easton)

1941 Harry S. Russell (Easton)

1946 J. Thomas Kibler (Chestertown)

1947 J. Thomas Kibler (Chestertown)

1948 Dallas Culver (Seaford)

1949 Fred Lucas (Cambridge)

Eastern Shore League Managers

Cambridge

1937 Fred Lucas

1938 Joe Davis

1939 Fred Lucas

1940 Hugh Poland

1941 Everett Johnston

1946 Jimmy Cooney & Barney DeForge

1947 Roy Nichols

1948 Bob Vickery & Stew Hofferth

1949 Merle Stracham

Centreville

1937 Joe O'Rourke

1938 Joe O'Rourke

1939 John Clark

1940 Ed Walls

1941 Ed Walls & Ed Popowski

1946 Jim McLeod

Crisfield

1937 Dan Pasquella & Bob Clark

Dover

1937 Ed Roetz & Jiggs Donahue

1938 Ray Brubaker

1939 Wes Kingdon & Walt Millies

1940 John Clark

1946 Hank Lehman

1947 Dick Carter

1948 Guy Glaser & Grover Wershing

Easton

1937 George Jacobs

1938 George Jacobs

1939 Ray Powell

1940 Ray Powell

1941 Dal Warren

1946 Jack Farmer

1947 Joe Antolick

1948 Joe Antolick

1949 Jack Farmer

Federalsburg

1937 George Short & John Tillman

1938 Charley Moss

1939 Sam Holbrook

1940 Sam Nisonoff

1941 Joe O'Rourke

1946 Lew Krausse

1947 Elmer Rambert

1948 Ducky Detweiler

1949 Carl McQuillen

Milford

1938 Val Picinich

1939 Val Picinich

1940 Bubber Jonnard

1941 Hal Gruber

1946 Walt Millies

1947 Walt Millies

1948 Clayton Sheedy

Pocomoke City

1937 Vic Keen

1938 Wes Kingdon

1939 Jake Flowers

1940 John Whalen

Rehoboth Beach

1947 Gordon McKinnon & Doug Peden

1948 Doug Peden

1949 Bill Sisler & John Watson

Salisbury

1937 Jake Flowers

1938 Jake Flowers

1939 Vic Keen & Spud Nachand

1940 Gus Brittain & Ed Kobesky

1941 John Wedemeyer & Bob Maier

1946 Harold Contini

1947 Harold Contini

1948 Gene Corbett

1949 Gene Corbett

Seaford

1946 Walter Youse & Joe Becker

1947 Bobby Westfall

1948 Harry Seibold

1949 Paul Gaulin

Index